## Other Books
## by Ralph H. Kilmann
## (*as author, coauthor, coeditor*)

The Management of Organization Design
Volume One: Strategies and Implementation

The Management of Organization Design
Volume Two: Research and Methodology

Social Systems Design:
Normative Theory and the MAPS Design Technology

Methodological Approaches to Social Science:
Integrating Divergent Concepts and Theories

Producing Useful Knowledge for Organizations

Beyond the Quick Fix:
Managing Five Tracks to Organizational Success

Corporate Tragedies:
Product Tampering, Sabotage, and Other Catastrophes

Gaining Control of the Corporate Culture

Corporate Transformation:
Revitalizing Organizations for a Competitive World

# Managing
# Beyond
# the
# Quick Fix

## A Completely
## Integrated Program
## for Creating
## and Maintaining
## Organizational Success

# Ralph H. Kilmann

## In Collaboration with
## Ines Kilmann

# Managing
# Beyond
# the
# Quick Fix

# A Completely
# Integrated Program
# for Creating
# and Maintaining
# Organizational Success

Jossey-Bass Publishers

San Francisco • London • 1989

MANAGING BEYOND THE QUICK FIX
*A Completely Integrated Program for Creating and Maintaining Organizational Success*
by Ralph H. Kilmann

Copyright © 1989 by: Jossey-Bass Inc., Publishers
350 Sansome Street
San Francisco, California 94104

&

Jossey-Bass Limited
28 Banner Street
London EC1Y 8QE

**Library of Congress Cataloging-in-Publication Data**

Kilmann, Ralph H.
  Managing beyond the quick fix : a completely integrated program for creating and maintaining organizational success / Ralph H. Kilmann in collaboration with Ines Kilmann.—1st ed.
      p.      cm.—(The Jossey-Bass management series)
  Bibliography: p.
  Includes index.
  ISBN 1-55542-132-6 (alk. paper)
  1. Organizational effectiveness.   2. Organizational change.
I. Kilmann, Ines.   II. Title.   III. Series.
HD58.9.K48      1989
658.4—dc19                                                              88-46084
                                                                            CIP

Manufactured in the United States of America

The paper in this book meets the guidelines for permanence and durability of the Committee on Production Guidelines for Book Longevity of the Council on Library Resources.

JACKET DESIGN BY WILLI BAUM

FIRST EDITION
    *First printing: February 1989*
    *Second printing: August 1989*

*Code 8905*

# The Jossey-Bass
# Management Series

*To my son*
*Christopher Martin Kilmann,*
*hoping that I will be as helpful to him*
*as my father has been to me*

# Contents

ix

# Preface

Organizations are the greatest invention of all time. They enable people to transcend their own limitations of both body and mind in order to manage the problems of nature and civilization. Without organized activity, all the other great inventions either would not have been created or would not have been brought to the marketplace. It is hardly an overstatement to suggest that economic prosperity and quality of life for the people of the world are largely determined by the functioning of organizations and institutions.

There are two fundamental questions that must be addressed in humanity's continuing struggle to improve its organizations and institutions: (1) What is the essence of organized activity—that is, what makes an organization successful? (2) How can this essence be managed—that is, how can organizational success be created and maintained?

Many people have tried to discover the essence of what makes an organization successful, whether it be an army, a church, a government, or an industrial corporation. Leavitt (1965), for example, developed one of the first frameworks for understanding the relationships among four organizational elements: task, structure, technology, and people. McKinsey and Company (Pascale and Athos, 1981) developed the 7-S framework to highlight seven interrelated elements—all beginning with the letter *s*: structure, systems, style, staff, skills, strategy, and shared values. Tichy (1983) developed the 3-Ropes framework to sort organizational theories into three intertwined strands: cultural, political, and technical. Most management textbooks now present a detailed framework for understanding the whole organization, which generally includes several well-accepted categories: environment, individuals, structures, processes, behavior, and outcomes (for example, see Gibson, Ivancevich, and Donnelly, 1988).

While considerable headway has been made in the past few decades in understanding the essence of organizational life, very little progress has been achieved with respect to *managing* that essence for organizational success. In most cases, those who advocate a particular framework have not provided any practical methods for managing organizations—as guided by their framework. Here the false assumption is that understanding the essence is the same thing as managing it: If managers are shown a conceptual framework, they will know what to do next. In some cases, the methods provided have focused almost exclusively on surface qualities that can be seen or touched directly—and can be changed quickly and easily as well. These methods do not stem from a deep understanding of the essence of organizations; they result from a cosmetic, expedient approach—to do something visible right away. Often referred to as the quick fix, some examples of this superficial tactic include redrawing the organizational chart, formulating a new strategic plan, establishing a quality control department, repainting an old office building, distributing a new list of corporate values, publicizing the importance of risk taking and innovation, and providing background music on the assembly line. Here the false assumption is that sight, sound, smell, taste, and touch—the five senses—are sufficient for understanding and managing the essence of organized activity. In the worst cases, not only do managers and consultants apply Band-Aids to their organizations, but they use only *one* approach while ignoring all the other interrelated aspects of the organization. Here the false assumption is that there exists one magic button that determines organizational success—if only one can find the right one to push.

This book provides a framework for understanding the essence of an organization *and* a completely integrated program for managing that essence for organizational success: I know of no other book that can make this claim.

With regard to understanding the essence of an organization, my framework identifies all the interrelated barriers that can interfere with creating and maintaining organizational success: the setting (dynamic complexity, external stakeholders), the organization (strategy-structure, reward system), the manager (management skills, problem management), the "third dimension" (culture, assumptions, psyches), the group (decision making, action taking), and the results (performance, morale).

With regard to managing the essence for organizational success, all the barriers between the setting (the environment outside the organization) and the psyche (the characteristics inside the individual) can be removed by implementing five tracks: (1) the culture track, (2) the management skills track, (3) the team-building track, (4) the strategy-structure track, and (5) the reward system track. The culture track enhances trust, communication, information sharing, and willingness to change among members—the conditions that must exist before any other improvement effort can succeed. The management skills track provides all management personnel with new ways of coping with complex problems and hidden assumptions. The team-building track infuses the new culture and updated management skills into each work unit—thereby instilling cooperation organization-wide so that complex problems can be addressed with all the expertise and information available. The strategy-structure track develops either a completely new or a revised strategic plan for the firm and then aligns divisions, departments, work groups, jobs, and all resources with the new strategic direction. The reward system track establishes a performance-based reward system that sustains all improvements by officially sanctioning the new culture, the use of updated management skills, and cooperative team efforts within and between all work groups.

The composition of the five tracks—consisting of techniques, instruments, and procedures that systematically remove the organization's barriers to success—represents the heart of a completely integrated program. But in order for the five tracks to provide their potential benefits, they must be surrounded by the critical stages of planned change—the body. Scheduling the five tracks for implementation, for example, must be preceded by obtaining top management's support and an accurate understanding of the organization's problems and opportunities. Implementing the five tracks, moreover, must be followed by assessing progress and making further adjustments to address what still needs attention. Therefore, a completely integrated program must combine the action levers that can remove all the organization's barriers to success with the ongoing activities required for managing systemwide change.

### Who Should Read This Book and Why

*Managing Beyond the Quick Fix* is written primarily for managers and consultants, although academics may find this material useful as well. Four key benefits derive from carefully reading and studying this book: (1) learning to see the world as a complex web of interpersonal, intergroup, interorganizational, and international relationships—and thereby understanding why quick fixes cannot result in long-term success; (2) learning to implement the five tracks—the core of the completely integrated program—as an important alternative to quick-fix thinking and behaving; (3) learning skills for distinguishing complex from simple problems, revising outdated assumptions about critical stakeholders (competitors, customers, employees), and defining problems correctly *before* solutions are chosen and implemented; and (4) learning about different personality types so that better use can be made of different experts, ideas, and insights—the key to defining and solving complex problems. These four learnings are essential for making any organization or institution more successful in today's competitive world.

Managers need to see how an integrated approach to organizational success can be undertaken. Managers and all members of an organization are often frustrated by the many barriers to success that block their efforts. In some cases, they feel helpless, inept, and out of control. The older the organization and the more single, cosmetic approaches for managing problems have been attempted, the more members are stymied by outdated cultures, ineffective management skills, poorly functioning work groups, ill-defined strategic objectives, bureaucratic red tape, and a reward system that does not reflect performance. But even organizations that are considered successful today may become unsuccessful tomorrow. The circumstances surrounding success can change radically without notice. In a fast-paced world, problems can develop overnight. All managers, therefore, must learn to identify barriers to success as they arise and then systematically remove them at the source—with a completely integrated program, not with more quick fixes.

Consultants need to update their skills for facilitating organizational success. They should not blindly and foolishly implement the single, cosmetic approaches that may have worked well in the past. In doing so, they would not be serving either their clients or their profession very well. Actually, I have found that most consultants apply their "pet" approaches, just as managers do. But this specialization simply will not work in today's interconnected world. Consultants must expand their range of skills and methods once they accept responsibility for implementing complete programs for long-term success rather than quick fixes for temporary relief.

Academics need to see how a wide variety of theories *and* methods can be combined into an integrated program of planned change, regardless of the reductionistic, theoretical habit of the social sciences. Perhaps this book will help academics develop other integrated programs for managing complex problems. Certainly, practitioners need these relevant programs much more than they need rigorous solutions to theoretical questions.

## Origin of This Book

The material in this book was developed during seventeen years of research, teaching, and consulting as a professor at the University of Pittsburgh. The first several years of this period resulted in the publication in 1977 of *Social Systems Design,* which outlined the integrated theories and methods of my approach to organizational success—understanding the essence. Although the 1977 book resulted in applications ranging from such organizations as General Electric, Gulf, and Xerox to such institutions as the U.S. Bureau of the Census and the Office of the President, several long-term efforts to implement all my ideas did not begin until 1980. With the publication in 1984 of *Beyond the Quick Fix,* more companies—both in the United States and abroad—began using my completely integrated program. It is because of these recent applications that I am able to report on the critical practices for *managing* beyond the quick fix—managing the essence. This volume captures what has been learned by translating theory into practice during the past five years.

The bibliography includes all my research publications that led to the writing of this book. I chose this form of documentation instead of giving extensive citations to my own work. Also, rather than give sentence-by-sentence citations from other authors just to add support to my propositions, I cite in the text only those works that pertain directly to a specific point. However, the bibliography includes a listing of the important publications that have influenced the direction of my thinking.

## Overview of the Contents

This book is one that must be studied, not skimmed—there is no way around it. I am not suggesting that the material is so difficult that it will take weeks and months to digest, but I do feel that it takes a thorough reading to learn what is being said. By skimming, one will miss the major points. I also ask the reader not to study the chapters out of order, as there is a certain building process that takes place. This is especially the case with the five tracks. They should be learned *and* implemented in the prescribed order.

The book is organized into eight chapters. Chapters One and Two summarize the key principles and practices underlying the completely integrated program. Chapter One, "Fundamental Principles for Improving Organizations," presents six key distinctions for the practice of management: (1) world as a complex hologram versus world as a simple machine, (2) complex versus simple problems, (3) multiple versus single approaches, (4) participative versus top-down management, (5) what managers can do with consultants versus without consultants, and (6) commitment to organizational success versus more quick fixes. As we will see, the first item in each of these six pairs represents what is necessary for creating and maintaining organizational success today, while the second item represents what was acceptable in the past.

Chapter Two, "Understanding the Completely Integrated Program," describes how managers, members, and consultants can join together to revitalize an organization for today's competitive world. The critical stages of planned change include initiating the program (making sure that the conditions for successful change are in place), diagnosing the problems (understanding all organizational barriers to success), scheduling the tracks (determining the techniques to be used in each track and the timing of the five tracks), implementing the tracks (adapting to a dynamic learning system with flexibility and imagination), and evaluating the results (measuring the impact of the program on the functioning of the organization and planning what to do next). Additional cycles of planned change unfold as the organization continues to adapt to environmental change: What began as a deliberate program of planned change during the first cycle evolves into a natural way of managing complexity in subsequent cycles.

Chapters Three through Seven detail the particular theory and methods that make up the five tracks, one track per chapter. These chapters are presented in the order in which the tracks need to be implemented: culture, management skills, team-building, strategy-structure, and reward systems. By following this sequence, all barriers to success are transformed into channels for success— thereby enabling the essence of the organization to flourish. Chapters Three through Seven, however, summarize only those methods that are best suited for managing *complex* problems and that have largely been ignored until recently. The other methods that can be sorted into the five tracks not only are well documented in the management literature but are best suited for solving *simple* problems.

Chapter Three presents "The Culture Track." Just as the concept of personality helps explain individual differences in attitude and behavior, the concept of culture helps explain organizational differences in decision making and action taking. The culture track uncovers the unwritten, unstated "norms" that guide each member's behavior within the organization: Don't disagree with your boss; don't make waves; treat women as second-class citizens; don't support the work of other groups; do the minimum to get by. Often, work groups pressure each member to follow such negative norms out of habit, which undermines trust, openness, and adaptiveness. The culture track first exposes the old culture and then, if necessary, creates a new culture. Without an adaptive culture, it is most difficult to engage in any other improvement effort. Thus, cultural barriers must be removed before proceeding with the other tracks.

Chapter Four presents "The Management Skills Track." This second track teaches managers how to define and solve complex problems by uncovering the underlying assumptions that drive all decisions into action. If these assumptions have remained unstated and therefore untested, managers may have continually made the wrong decisions. Managers may have unknowingly assumed: No new competitors will enter the industry; the government will protect the domestic marketplace; consumers will buy whatever the firm produces; employees will continue to accept current working conditions. In short, all previous decisions may have been based more on fantasy and habit than on reality and choice. Outdated assumptions may have steered the organization into adopting the wrong strategy-structure and reward system as well. With a new culture that encourages trust and openness, however, members will be able to examine their previously unstated assumptions before crucial problems are defined and any critical decisions are made. No longer will the members be held back by their own faulty assumptions.

Chapter Five presents "The Team-Building Track." The third track infuses the new cultural norms and the new management skills into every work unit and between work units. Without concerted effort to transfer all that is learned in workshops (during the first two tracks) to the workplace, any short-term improvements will quickly disappear (the fate of all quick fixes). Included in this track is a method for controlling the organization's troublemakers—individuals who continually restrict cooperative efforts through their self-serving, disruptive behavior. As the troublemakers are put in check, each work group learns to approach its business and technical problems with its new culture and skills. Gradually, well-functioning teams replace old-fashioned cliques. Then the focus shifts to identifying and resolving interdepartmental conflicts that interfere with organizational success.

Chapter Six presents "The Strategy-Structure Track." Once the first three tracks have removed the cultural, skill, and group barriers to success (the informal organization), the fourth track examines two formally documented systems in the organization: Strategy first sets the firm's direction; structure then organizes specific objectives, tasks, people, and resources into action—for each work unit and each job in the organization. Determining the correct alignment of strategy and structure is, perhaps, one of the most crucial problems facing the organization. If this problem is not solved correctly, where is the organization headed and how will it get there? Only if the earlier tracks have been implemented properly will the necessary culture, skills, and cooperative efforts be available for addressing strategy and structure in a forthright, systematic, and comprehensive manner.

Chapter Seven presents "The Reward System Track." The fifth track makes sure that members are appropriately rewarded for performing the right tasks with the right objectives in mind. It will become clear, however, that conducting this last track is futile if all the other tracks have not been managed properly. Without an adaptive culture, members will not believe that rewards are tied to performance. Instead, they will believe that it is useless to work hard and do well. Similarly, if managers do not have the skills required to conduct performance appraisal, any well-intentioned reward system will be thwarted. If the work groups in the organization do not tolerate individual differences, it will be most difficult for managers to distinguish high and low performers—which is what every pay-for-performance system must do. Furthermore, if the strategy and structure of the organization are not developed and aligned correctly, the reward system cannot measure performance objectively. The reward system, therefore, is the last major barrier to success to be removed—typically the "bottom line" for the organization's members.

Chapter Eight presents "Managing the Completely Integrated Program." Having presented in the previous five chapters a detailed discussion of the theories and methods in each of the five tracks, it is important to return again to the holistic perspective offered in this book—to put it all together. Managing beyond the quick fix requires an integrated use of individual, group, and organizational activities, which can only be fully appreciated using a live example. Experiencing the complete program is always full of complex surprises. The plan never takes place as intended. This concluding chapter presents the story of the Eastman Kodak Company, where the complete program was implemented for the corporate function of market intelligence. The purpose of this function—consisting of some 125 information specialists—is to provide quality information for making important decisions for Kodak's lines of business. This case illustrates how an energized corporate function, with matrix ties to the rest of the company, can serve as the central nervous system for quality decision making and action taking throughout a large, multinational corporation.

*Pittsburgh, Pennsylvania*                              Ralph H. Kilmann
*January 1989*

# Acknowledgments

This book is an integration of my personal life and my professional career. Many people and institutions, therefore, have significantly affected the final product. I would like to express special appreciation to those who have shaped my identity and my ideas.

Both my parents, Lilli and Martin Kilmann, have instilled in me a sense of purpose and a desire to learn. My mother introduced me to classical music, which developed my feelings; my father introduced me to the game of chess, which developed my thinking. My mother, the homemaker, taught me integrity and perseverance; my father, the ophthalmologist, taught me what it means to be a professional. My brother, Peter, provided the emotional support and the psychological insights I needed to understand myself and others—especially during difficult times. My grandmother, Helena, gave me the unconditional love that only a grandparent can give. My uncle, Morris, gave me the opportunity to see an entrepreneur in action, which planted the seed for my career interests in management and organizations. All my children,

Cathy, Christopher, and Arlette, continue to inspire my introspection and appreciate my choices.

Outside my family, my educational and job experiences have been varied, and several were significant: Richard Novie taught me graphic arts in eighth grade. Frank Neubauer further encouraged this interest when he, as president of Transkrit Corporation, hired me to work as an apprentice in his printing factory during my summers in high school. My growing appreciation for the dissemination of knowledge through the printed word determined my choice of college: Carnegie Institute of Technology (now Carnegie Mellon University). At Carnegie, I majored in graphic arts management, not yet realizing that I would enjoy writing words even more than printing them. When I was contemplating whether to take a management job in the graphic arts industry upon completing my Master of Science degree at Carnegie's Graduate School of Industrial Administration, Professor Kenneth Mackenzie suggested that I go into research instead. He said that I enjoyed creating and integrating ideas more than anything else. He was absolutely right. The next semester, I enrolled in the doctoral program in management at the University of California, Los Angeles (UCLA).

The radically different philosophies of learning in my two graduate programs significantly shaped my understanding of the whole and my appreciation of the different parts. At Carnegie, if you did not understand something, it was because you had not taken enough courses in mathematics—particularly calculus. At UCLA, if you did not understand something, it was because you needed more psychological counseling—particularly psychoanalysis. Between these two extremes, I learned that there is always more than one way to look at something, whether it be philosophy, science, or a complex business problem. I also learned that a more complete understanding of the whole is possible only by accepting the idea that each extreme is right—from a certain point of view.

A very large door was opened for me when Raghu Nath at the University of Pittsburgh (Pitt) contacted Bill McKelvey at UCLA in order to screen doctoral students for a new faculty position. As a result of this one telephone call, my first university job interview took place at Pitt's Graduate School of Business in

June 1971. Following this interview, I chose to begin my career at Pitt because Dean Jerry Zoffer promised me unlimited resources and complete freedom to pursue my career—and such a grandiose offer was extended even before I had begun my dissertation or published a single article. Seventeen years later, I can say unequivocally that he came through on his promise. For some unknown reason, he believed in me and acted accordingly.

Several social scientists have affected my personal and professional development in significant ways: Chris Argyris, Warren Bennis, Colleen Carney, West Churchman, Dave Jamieson, Robert Kelley, Ed Lawler, Ken Mackenzie, Ian Mitroff, Tom Saaty, Bob Tannenbaum, Tuck Taylor, Ken Thomas, and Jerry Zaltman. Several former doctoral students have supported my efforts as well: Larry Boone, Teresa Joyce Covin, Dick Herden, Bernie Jaworski, Bob Keim, Marjorie Lyles, Walt McGhee, Debbie MacInnis, Mary Jane Saxton, Joe Seltzer, and Dave Wood. Several executives have encouraged me to continue improving the application of my theories and methods: Vince Barabba, Pedro Grau, Peter Mathias, Bill Peace, Roy Serpa, and Don Utter. Special appreciation is given to Shafiq Naz, who has been very supportive of my work and of my desire to interact with people of different cultures.

The Eastman Kodak Company plays a unique role in this book, because they agreed to let me make public the application of the completely integrated program to their organization. Vince Barabba, director of Market Intelligence, initiated the program in 1984 and then, in the midst of implementing the fourth track, passed the baton to Bill Lawton. While a change in leadership often upsets the implementation of an improvement effort, in the Kodak case, the activities of the program never skipped a beat. Bill Hales and Barbara Young were very helpful in organizing and conducting different aspects of implementation.

My administrative assistant, Camille Burgess, carefully completes everything I possibly can delegate to her. My long-term assistant, Jeanette Engel, always asks if there is anything else she can do for me. Jossey-Bass people delivered their usual first-class performance under the superb leadership of Steve Piersanti. My editor, Bill Hicks, provided the impetus for this book when one day he asked me: "Did you ever think about writing a new book about everything you have learned since we first published *Beyond the Quick Fix?"*

Finally, and most important, a very special acknowledgment is given to the one person who collaborated with me on every aspect of this book: Ines Kilmann. Her practical work experience in a wide variety of management positions has been invaluable in helping me discover the essence of my work and make it more accessible to a management audience. She has been willing to create ideas, analyze concepts, and critique chapters at any time of the day or night. Ines brings out the best in me.

# The Author

Ralph H. Kilmann is professor of business administration and director of the Program in Corporate Culture at the Joseph M. Katz Graduate School of Business, University of Pittsburgh. He received both his B.S. and M.S. degrees in industrial administration from Carnegie Mellon University (1970) and his Ph.D. in management from the University of California, Los Angeles (1972). Kilmann is a member of the Academy of Management, the American Psychological Association, and the Institute of Management Sciences. He serves on the editorial boards of *Academy of Management Executive, Journal of Management,* and *Journal of Organizational Change Management.*

Kilmann has published more than one hundred articles and books on such topics as organizational design, strategy, structure, and culture; conflict management; organizational effectiveness; organizational change and development; defining and solving complex problems; interpersonal and small-group behavior; and the design and functioning of scientific institutions. He is a biographee in Marquis's *Who's Who in the World, Who's Who in*

*Finance and Industry,* and *Who's Who in Frontiers of Science and Technology.*

Kilmann is the developer of the MAPS Design Technology, a computer-based method for redesigning organizations. This technology has been used for designing management information systems, identifying and solving organization-wide problems, developing strategic intelligence systems, and redesigning the operating divisions of major product groups and functional areas. He has developed several diagnostic instruments for assessing individual and organizational characteristics: the Kilmann Insight Test, the Learning Climate Questionnaire, and the Thomas-Kilmann Conflict Mode Instrument. Recently, he developed the Kilmann-Saxton Culture-Gap Survey to assess the unspoken cultural norms in organizations, to identify the gaps between actual and desired norms, and, thereby, to pinpoint the directions for developing a more adaptive corporate culture.

Since 1975, Kilmann has been president of Organizational Design Consultants, a Pittsburgh-based firm specializing in the five tracks to organizational success. His corporate clients include AT&T, Eastman Kodak, Ford, General Electric, General Foods, TRW, Westinghouse, and Xerox. In addition, Kilmann has applied his methods for planned change to health care organizations, financial service companies, and government institutions, including the U.S. Bureau of the Census and the Office of the President.

# Managing
# Beyond
# the
# Quick Fix

## A Completely
## Integrated Program
## for Creating
## and Maintaining
## Organizational Success

# 1

# Fundamental Principles
# for Improving Organizations

American management, especially in the two decades after World War II, was universally admired for its striking effective performance. But times change. An approach shaped and refined during stable decades may be ill suited to a world characterized by rapid and unpredictable change, scarce energy, global competition for markets, and a constant need for innovation. This is the world of the 1980s and, probably, the rest of this century.

—Hayes and Abernathy, 1980, p. 68

The world has become increasingly accessible—resulting from the computer revolution, the information explosion, and telecommunications. With a personal computer, modem, telephone, and television (with its round-the-clock Cable News Network), the world is at one's fingertips. Back in the 1950s, the world seemed to become smaller due to air travel. Now the world is even smaller and more accessible due to information travel.

At the same time, the world has become increasingly interconnected—resulting from both the deregulation of many industries and the competition for world markets. The stock market crash in October 1987 painfully demonstrated that nations and their economies are no longer isolated and protected as they were in the

1

past. Everyone in the industrialized world witnessed how the market expectations of one nation affected dramatically the behavior of other nations—all over the world, instantly.

Most organizations today exist under these conditions of worldwide accessibility and worldwide interconnectedness: Almost everything changes quickly in unpredictable ways—with unanticipated rippling effects on almost everything else. This "dynamic complexity" means that organizations cannot remain stable for very long. Rather, constant change on the outside requires constant change on the inside. Creating and maintaining organizational success is largely determined by how well managers adjust all the interrelated aspects of their organization to keep it on track with its surroundings.

The older and larger a firm, the more trouble it has changing. Essentially, the organization becomes rigidified. Just as hardening of the arteries sets in with age for individuals, hardening of the documents (and assumptions and culture) comes with age and size for organizations. Making matters worse, if the organization has been successful in the past, its managers may fall into the trap of "erroneous extrapolation." This occurs when managers make the false assumption that what worked in the last decade will work in the next. Thus some managers draw a straight line from the past into the future. With dynamic complexity as the new rule, however, the past does *not* flow smoothly into the future. Instead, it is more likely that the future will be fundamentally different from the past. In some cases, the very thing that brought the organization its past success will bring about its eventual downfall.

The temptation for both managers and consultants is to gravitate toward the single approach that offers the promise of organizational success. In today's world, however, single approaches are typically knee-jerk reactions to whatever ails the organization at that moment—the quick fixes or Band-Aids that are applied directly to the symptom of the problem. If members complain about a lack of direction, top executives institute a new strategic planning system. If there is a need for more innovation, top executives announce a special-recognition program for new product ideas. If morale is low, as indicated by the latest employee-opinion survey, top executives publicize the company's new sports program. No effort is made to find out how all the other interrelated aspects of the organization—such as outdated cultures, ineffective management skills, poorly functioning work groups, bureaucratic red tape, and a reward system that ignores performance—may be contributing to the problem. Boyle (1983, p. 22) aptly describes the Band-Aid style used by managers in most organizations:

> This reactive style responds to each problem in the organization as if it were an isolated phenomenon. Instead of preventing fires, it's always fighting fires. Because it favors the quick fix over the long-term solution, it may not be fixing the right thing at all. Because there isn't any process in place that allows the organization to anticipate the need for change before a crisis breaks, it is always one step behind the times.

The time has come to resist the lure of the next quick fix. We must make sure that we do not fall prey to its trap—one more time. The danger of the quick fix is slowly being recognized, but the necessary defenses to ward off the temptation are not yet firmly ingrained in the ways managers think and act. This clinging belief in the quick fix is demonstrated—once again—by the new wave of gurus who have entered the corporate arena. As reported in a *Fortune* article, their promise, simply put, is quick personal and organizational transformation (Main, 1987, p. 95):

> In their occasionally feverish effort to become more competitive, American businessmen have grabbed for one restorative after another, some of them quite strange. None seems stranger than the human potential movement, which for years has offered the ordinary citizen a vaguely defined "breakthrough experience": In a weekend or so, change your life forever. Now prophets of the movement have begun to argue that they can fundamentally change companies the same way, by appealing to emotions rather than reason. The gurus have adapted their standard programs to suit business clients and are finding a fast-growing market among

corporations still searching for *the* answer to productivity problems.

Not surprisingly, when managers in all nations are asked what can be done to transform their organizations into adaptive, market-driven, innovative, and competitive systems, their usual reply conveys that they are still waiting for the right quick fix to come along. Most are not aware of any alternatives to the quick fix. Nobody even knows for sure what to call "it" other than a *non-quick fix*. Certainly, one important step in the right direction is to question the long-held assumptions about planned change: Can our organizations be revitalized? Are methods now available that can tackle such a complex arrangement of culture, skills, teams, strategy, structures, and reward systems? This book answers *yes*—if managers can unlearn their old ways and are willing to adopt a new way of managing the dynamic complexity around them.

### The Six Principles

Six key principles highlight why a completely integrated program is essential for organizational success and why quick fixes inevitably lead to failure. The first principle recognizes that managers must *see* the world in a new way—as a complex hologram—before they can think and act differently. The second principle suggests why complex, interrelated problems emerge from this new worldview. The third principle indicates why multiple approaches must be implemented in order to solve complex problems effectively. The fourth principle tells why only participative management can hope to bring forth the relevant knowledge and member acceptance needed to implement multiple approaches effectively. The fifth principle explains why internal and external consultants should be used for those aspects of an improvement program that managers cannot or should not do on their own. The sixth principle emphasizes why long-term organizational success cannot be achieved unless top management fully commits to a completely integrated program of planned change.

In essence, the six principles describe key contrasts between what may have worked in the past and what is needed now. If these principles are not fully appreciated and fully understood, managers will not even recognize the many interrelated barriers to success. More important, without *acting* on these principles, managers will not be able to transform all barriers—via an integrated program of planned change—into channels for success. Barriers will continue to hold the organization back, whereas channels will provide the opportunity to move forward. Whether the organization is beset with barriers or blessed with channels is very much top management's choice.

### Principle 1: World as a Complex Hologram Versus World as a Simple Machine

The need for a completely integrated program is lodged in the new kind of world in which we live. Three types of worldview can be distinguished: the world as a simple machine, the world as an open system, and the world as a complex hologram (Mitroff and Kilmann, 1984a).

The first worldview, a simple machine, argues for single efforts at change, much like replacing one defective part in some mechanical apparatus: The one defective part can be replaced without affecting any other part. This single approach works only for fixing a physical, nonliving system. The quick fix cannot hope to heal a human being, much less a living, breathing organization. The simple machine view represents one-dimensional thinking— much like studying the world as a collection of isolated cities.

The second worldview, the open system, argues for a more integrated approach in which several parts must be balanced simultaneously in order to manage the whole organization. Here a dynamic equilibrium exists between an organization and its changing environment. The organization consists of systems, such as strategies, structures, and rewards. The environment contains its own systems, too, such as the government, suppliers, competitors, and consumers. This worldview, however, focuses just on the surface, where things can be easily observed and measured. The open system represents two-dimensional thinking—much like studying the world with a flat map.

The third worldview, the complex hologram, adds depth to the open system—analogous to forming a three-dimensional image by reflecting beams of light at different angles. The complex hologram includes the interrelated, at-the-surface aspects of the open system *plus* the interrelated, below-the-surface aspects that are often overlooked. Thus the complex hologram probes below the surface to examine *culture* (shared but unwritten rules for each member's behavior), *assumptions* (unquestioned beliefs behind all decisions and actions), and *psyches* (the deepest reaches of the mind). The complex hologram represents three-dimensional thinking—much like studying the world with a relief map and with X-rays and sonar as well.

Figure 1 shows a graphic representation of the three worldviews. The simple machine is shown as neatly arranged squares; the shaded areas represent defective parts to be replaced quickly, while the environment and all other parts are ignored. The open system is shown with the environment (E) and the directly observable aspects of the organization, all interrelated in a network. The complex hologram is portrayed by adding the dimension of depth—what is not directly observable—to the open system.

**Figure 1. Three Worldviews.**

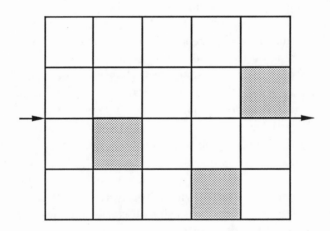

**A. The Simple Machine.**

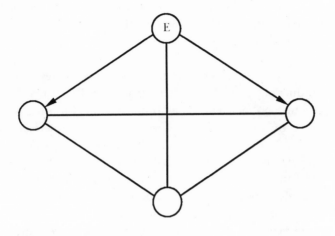

**B. The Open System.**

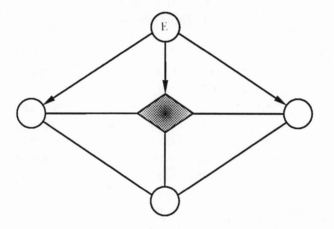

**C. The Complex Hologram.**

I believe the simple machine view of the world is already outdated. It had its heyday in the industrial revolution back in the eighteenth and nineteenth centuries. Yet looking at the way contemporary organizations are designed and managed would lead one to conclude that the simple machine conception is still alive and well: Quick fixes are all around us! Managers continue to search for the timeless fantasy of simplicity, perfection, and certainty. Rose (1983, p. 84) summarizes the historical foundation of the simple machine view of the world:

> More than any other country, the United States is a product of classical science, the science of Newton and Descartes, the science that produced the Enlightenment and the Industrial Revolution. The American political system is based on the Newtonian view of the universe as a clocklike mechanism of separate parts all working together under immutable laws. John Locke's notion of the free individual existing under natural law, Adam Smith's conception of the invisible hand at work in a free marketplace—these are ideas that follow directly from the Newtonian conception of an orderly and mechanical world. But, unfortunately, the world is not that simple [anymore].

The complex hologram—adding a variety of hidden and unconscious forces to the interconnectedness of the open system— seems to capture the essence of the world today. Thus the complex hologram represents the most compelling approach when complexity, imperfection, and uncertainty are the norm—a three-dimensional view of life beyond the five senses. Capra (1982, pp. 19–20), for example, believes that we *must* replace the simple machine view of the world with a more holographic approach. Otherwise, it will be nearly impossible to manage the constant stream of social and environmental threats to our planet's survival—such as crime, violence, pollution, disease, poverty, and nuclear war:

> All of these threats are actually different facets of one and the same crisis—essentially a crisis of perception. We are trying to apply the concepts of an outdated worldview—the mechanistic worldview of Cartesian-Newtonian science—to a reality that can no longer be understood in these terms.
>     We live in a globally interconnected world, in which biological, psychological, social, and environ-

mental phenomena are all interdependent. To describe this world appropriately we need an ecological
perspective that the Cartesian worldview cannot offer.

What we need, then, is a fundamental change
in our thoughts, perceptions, and values. The begin-
nings of this change are already visible in all fields,
and the shift from a mechanistic to a holistic conception of reality is likely to dominate the entire decade.
The gravity and global extent of our crisis indicate
that the current changes are likely to result in a
transformation of unprecedented dimensions, a turning point for the planet as a whole.

Lest the reader conclude that the dichotomy between the
simple machine and the complex hologram is relevant only to
social and organizational problems, consider Slater's (1974, pp. 29-
30) critique of the practice of medicine:

It has taken more than a century for Western medicine
to rediscover what witch doctors and shamans have
known all along: (1) that a disease occurs in the whole
organism, not, as in a machine, in one defective part;
and (2) that every organism is organically related to
others, and to the total environment, and hence any
"cure" that does not take account of these relationships is likely to be ephemeral. What we stigmatize as
magic is scientific inasmuch as it teaches the whole-
ness and interconnectedness of living forms. Scientific
medicine, on the other hand, is irrational in that it
treats the organism as if it were a machine, discon-
nected from its surroundings and internally dis-
connectable.

Managers and consultants—all healers of human systems—
will not become successful by tinkering with the parts. A vastly
different approach is necessary. Organizations must be viewed as
holographic images. Otherwise, managers, consultants, and academics will see only a small portion of the total picture. If managers

work with just the simple machine parts of the organization, they will be severely limited in what they can accomplish in today's world. If consultants examine just these parts, they too will be unable to help managers address their problems. If academics see the organization with the same blinders, they will find it impossible to explain much of what goes on in organizations. Without the holographic view, most of what goes on and must be managed for success would be beyond everyone's perceptual reach.

### Principle 2: Complex Versus Simple Problems

While conducting executive management programs throughout the world, I make use of a thought-provoking exercise that helps the participants see the interrelationships among worldviews, organizations, and problems. First, I ask the participants to sort their organizations into the three categories of simple machine, open system, and complex hologram according to which metaphor best illustrates how their organizations function. Again and again, at least 75 percent of the participants indicate that their companies are being run as a simple machine! Then I ask them to list all their major organizational problems. Next I ask them to sort these problems into the same three categories: simple machine, open system, and complex hologram. To their surprise, almost all their problems are sorted into the complex hologram. In fact, rarely does anyone list a major organizational problem that fits the category of simple machine! Through this exercise, the great majority of managers arrive at the conclusion that most of their organizations are designed to manage simple problems while few of their problems are of this variety.

A problem is simple when one person has all the expertise and information to solve it. In solving such a problem, it is unnecessary to bring in additional experts who have the same knowledge—extra persons could not improve the quality of the decision. For example, any qualified accountant would have all the necessary expertise and information to select the right method for costing a firm's inventory.

A problem is complex, alternatively, when one person *cannot* have all the expertise and information to solve it. This deficiency stems from people's limited capacity to store vast amounts of information and acquire widely different areas of expertise. Simply put, each person tends to be a specialist in only one or, at most, a few areas. Complex problems, however, involve many different angles—as in a complex hologram—and require many diverse competencies. Thus several different experts must interact in order to develop a high-quality decision. The group determining the firm's new strategic direction, for example, should include a variety of specialists from each division, department, and staff group in the organization plus others who understand the economy, competitors, government agencies, and public opinion.

An interesting way to distinguish simple from complex problems is by making use of the old Indian story about the six blind men and the elephant. A simple problem can be illustrated as six men, each of whom has perfect 20/20 vision *and* an unobstructed view of the whole elephant. If these six men were asked to indicate what they see, all of them would probably say "elephant." Since each one is able to see the whole animal perfectly, the six individual viewpoints are redundant.

A complex problem, alternatively, can be illustrated as six blind men, each standing directly in front of a different portion of the elephant. As each man is asked to indicate what he perceives— using senses other than sight—there is considerable disagreement concerning the beast before them. If these six men do not appreciate that each has a different perspective to contribute, a close-minded argument continues without reaching the right conclusion. Only if the six blind men recognize their differences and *integrate* their sensory experiences into a whole image will they reach the surprising conclusion that the creature before them is indeed an elephant. In this case, each person has a unique view of the whole and needs the different insights from the others to solve the problem.

With increasing dynamic complexity outside organizations and with greater individual specialization inside organizations, each person has a more limited view of a whole product or service. Consequently, only by recognizing and appreciating different areas of knowledge can organizational members manage the complex "beasts" they encounter in a holographic world.

*Principle 3: Multiple Versus Single Approaches*

Single approaches can solve simple problems; multiple approaches can manage complex problems. It would be inefficient—a waste of time and resources—to use a multiple approach when the problem is simple. It would be ineffective, however, to attempt to solve a complex problem with a single approach—the problem could not be solved regardless of the efficiency of the effort. Attempting to implement a new strategic plan by inadvertently ignoring all the corresponding changes in culture, skills, structure, and reward systems needed to make the new plan work, for example, is doomed to fail.

A multiple approach to organizational success must include a variety of leverage points in order to control—hence manage— performance and morale. A *leverage point* is anything that a manager can change in the organization, such as rules, procedures, objectives, and the acquisition of skills. The principle of multiple approaches is demonstrated by the five tracks: (1) the culture track, (2) the management skills track, (3) the team-building track, (4) the strategy-structure track, and (5) the reward system track. These tracks are designed to remove the full range of at-the-surface and below-the-surface barriers to organizational success. Each track consists of specific leverage points for use by managers and consultants.

Furthermore, as a result of the interconnectedness of every aspect of the organization, the five tracks must be conducted in sequence—(1) through (5)—as multiple, *integrated* leverage points. The first track develops a culture to foster trust, communication, information sharing, and willingness to change among members— the qualities needed to proceed with all other improvement efforts. During the second track, all managers learn new skills for solving complex problems. In particular, they learn the methods for uncovering and then updating assumptions; without a supportive culture, managers would keep their assumptions under lock and key. The third track enables each work group to make daily use of the new culture and updated skills for solving important business problems; gradually, former cliques become effective teams. The fourth track guides these effective teams to address two of the most important yet most sensitive problems an organization can face: its own strategy and structure. Once the organization and all its members are moving in the right direction, the fifth track designs a reward system to sustain high performance and morale into the future. Naturally, the organization's functioning must be examined periodically to evaluate whether fine tuning is needed in any of the tracks. Any external changes in the organization's setting may require corresponding internal adjustments, and the cycle of planned change continues.

Multiple approaches to organizational success, therefore, mean influencing all the organization's surface aspects and its cultural, assumptional, and psychological aspects. This point is so fundamental that it cannot be overstated. I consider it foolhardy for managers and consultants to try to solve today's interconnected problems with a single approach that uses only one leverage point.

### Principle 4: Participative Versus Top-Down Management

Most people are willing to lend a helping hand if asked courteously and sincerely. People enjoy contributing to a worthwhile cause. If there are significant problems requiring extensive cooperation on everyone's part, generating a team spirit will go far toward overcoming barriers and solving problems. Only in a crisis, when time is limited, is a different kind of approach called for.

It seems that viewing the world as a simple machine, however, creates organizations in the mold of the Prussian army. The terminology itself—chain of command, lines of authority, span of control, line versus staff—has its roots in military organizations. Here one salutes the uniform and not the man. The officers are wise and all-knowing; the recruits are ignorant and just waiting to be told what to do—there to do, not to think. Stephen Vincent Benét (1927, p. 12) described the dilemma of the military model as follows:

> If you take a flat map and move wooden blocks upon it strategically, the thing looks well, the blocks behave as they should. The science of war is moving live men like blocks. And getting the blocks into place at a fixed moment. But it takes time to mold your men into

blocks. And flat maps turn into country where creeks
and gullies hamper your wooden squares. They stick
in the brush, they are tired and rest, they straggle over
ripe blackberries, and you cannot lift them up in your
hand and move them.

Top-down management seems very akin to the military
model in its style and assumptions. Managers behave as if one-way
communication, backed by the formal authority of their position, is
enough to implement any decision. The assumption is that members lower down in the hierarchy will understand what is intended
and follow through exactly as requested—like moving blocks on a
flat map. If the decision is a simple instruction to be carried out,
perhaps a top-down approach is fine. If the members are eager to do
whatever those above them request, perhaps their compliance is
automatic. If they have· learned never to question their superiors,
then again they are likely to comply.

When trying to define the complex barriers to success that are
holding the organization back, top managers do not have a
monopoly on expertise and information. The nature of complexity,
as we have seen, is that one person cannot possibly have all the
relevant insight to solve the problem. Taking the top executive
group as just one perspective suggests that every complex problem
needs the additional perspectives of the lower-level managers and
employees.

Moreover, the extent to which decisions require *commitment*
for successful implementation suggests that the lower-level
members may not comply automatically. If they do not commit to
the improvement program as intended, what finally is implemented
may be a far cry from what top management had in mind. Likewise,
an improvement program may not be implemented successfully
because members interpret top management's message as "commit
to the program when and as you see fit." It never fails to amaze me
how many times the lower-level members look the other way as they
interpret the latest improvement effort in this light.

The alternative to top-down management is the participative
approach. Here members throughout the organization are involved
in decision making and implementation on matters that directly

concern them. Since members at the lower levels are generally closest to the machinery, the consumer, and the community, they are in an excellent position to observe problems and offer different viewpoints. Their involvement in decision making also creates the commitment necessary for successful implementation. If members throughout the organization have been directly involved in diagnosing the full range of barriers to success, for example, it is likely that they will commit to an improvement program that is designed to remove these obstacles.

In a holographic world that elicits complex problems continuously, not only are completely integrated programs for planned change required but these programs must be conducted in a participative manner. This is the only style for collecting information that is likely to produce high-quality decisions and employees' commitment to implement these decisions. Participative management, therefore, is advocated not because of some social value or ethical imperative, but because it is the only way to solve a complex problem.

### Principle 5: What Managers Can Do
### With Consultants Versus Without Consultants

Complex problems demand a broad range of expertise and information. With a participative approach, the organization has full access to all its members. Is that enough? I do not think so, especially since we are examining something as complex as organizational change. What if the members affected by the problem do not have all the necessary ingredients to proceed? Should management search outside its boundaries? Certainly. For its most important problems, the organization should not restrict itself to the talents and insights of only the membership.

Let us define two types of consultants: internal and external. Internal consultants are employed full time by the organization and reside in various staff groups or in a department of human resources, personnel, organizational development, quality improvement, corporate development, or organizational planning. Any of these departments may include people who are trained in diagnosing and solving organizational problems—working on either business-related problems with technical expertise or systems-related problems with management expertise.

An external consultant, as the distinction suggests, is not an employee of the company. Such consultants are drawn from consulting firms, independent practice, or university settings. These experts may not have an intimate knowledge of the business side of the organization. But they are probably more objective in their approach because of their temporary contractual relationship with the organization.

External consultants are needed most when top management wants to collect information about problems the membership experiences—particularly if these problems involve the way the organization is managed. It is very unlikely that members will be completely candid with their superiors about delicate matters before a healthy, open culture is functioning. Even internal consultants may have difficulty in getting members to disclose their true opinions for fear that this information could travel back to their bosses. Even if anonymous questionnaires are used as a way of collecting members' perceptions, some people will still be reluctant to present their true feelings. Indeed, they may fear that their questionnaires are coded somehow to identify respondents. Therefore, both managers and internal consultants may be unable to gather diagnostic information when the topic—management and organizational problems—is too close to home.

An external consultant, however, is more likely to develop the rapport with the membership necessary to gather such information. Naturally, confidentiality must be stressed and precautions must be taken. But external consultants are in the best position to argue for trust, confidence, and sincerity because of their independent position.

Besides collecting delicate information regarding the diagnosis of the organization's problems, consultants (either internal or external) are better than managers at dealing with interpersonal problems, group feedback sessions, and troublemakers. These topics always bring ego defenses and psychological problems to the forefront. It takes a specially trained consultant to work with these delicate aspects of human nature. Likewise, consultants are better than managers at bringing the hidden cultures to the surface, since these cultures may not portray what top management was hoping to learn. Similarly, consultants may be best at guiding the process that uncovers hidden assumptions. Often a fair amount of stress is involved when managers first see their outmoded assumptions face-to-face. A skilled consultant is needed to help managers work through such confronting moments.

Weinshall (1982, pp. 53–54), in an article titled "Help for Chief Executives: The Outside Consultant," eloquently summarizes why managers cannot conduct planned change all by themselves:

> The question is whether managements need, and can be helped by, outside consultants. . . . The answer to this question is definitely in the affirmative. Managements in all organizations suffer from a condition referred to as the "no-full-disclosure disease." This disease manifests itself through people within the managerial hierarchy who do not reveal to their colleagues all their concerns about the organization. They worry that the things threatening them may come to the notice of those who affect their position in the organization. They worry that their immediate superior may hear things which will be detrimental to their own advancement or beneficial to the promotion of others. They worry about their peers, with whom they compete for the favor of a common superior. They worry about their subordinates, younger and more recently trained and educated, whose acquired knowledge of the organization may soon rival their own and thus destroy their own area of superiority. . . .
>
> The no-full-disclosure disease is a universal one and no organization is free from it. Most managers who first hear of its universality are surprised, thinking that it only affects their organization and themselves—a phenomenon known as the "fallacy of uniqueness." This disease is the cause of grave pathologies among managements, referred to as "undisclosed feelings" and the "hierarchical com-

munication gap." Curing these ailments, and the no-full-disclosure disease which causes them, can be done only by outside consultants, who can help managers to open up, [and] bridge the communication gap.

If all managers realized that the world has changed and they can no longer expect to be on top of every situation, perhaps this might relieve some of the pressure. It might encourage them to collaborate, to seek more help from the membership, from internal and external consultants, from the community—in short, from anyone anywhere. This is the name of the game in a holographic world. The age-old values of self-sufficiency and independence must be replaced with reciprocity and *inter*dependence.

### Principle 6: Commitment to Organizational Success Versus More Quick Fixes

Multiple approaches—with the use of participation and consultants—have the potential to revitalize our organizations. Now top managers must do the rest: commit the time, energy, and resources to pinpoint all the barriers to success and transform them into channels for success. Will top managers commit beyond the quick fix?

Commitment to act—to put oneself on the line, to risk failure and humiliation—is a tough decision. Most people are reluctant to commit themselves fully to anything, whether it be another person, an idea, or an integrated solution to a complex problem. To understand the dynamics of commitment in a holographic world, we must probe below the surface to examine the roots of personal responsibility.

Perhaps one of our greatest fears is that we will be held responsible for some outcome that can hurt other people. This fear seems to derive from the egocentricity of children: At an early age, children believe they are the center of the universe, that all life revolves around them. Even events beyond their control seem to result from their idle thoughts or their innocent actions. Children feel they are responsible for everything.

As children develop into adults, they learn to distinguish

cause from effect and to separate what they have done (and consequently are responsible for) from what was done by others, caused by nature, or induced by other forces. Through everyday experience and formal training, the adult learns physics, chemistry, biology, economics, and psychology—the cause-and-effect sciences that explain everyday experience. What we cannot explain we assign to superstition, chance, and religion.

Most people, however, do not make the full transition from egocentric child who believes in magic to renaissance adult who knows all science. Instead, most people worry about the consequences of doing something wrong, unintentionally causing harm to other people, or being punished for having caused an unhappy outcome. Some people are so afraid of being held responsible that they do not act. Others are willing to act as long as they can blame someone else for the results—or any other external source that is convenient.

Accepting responsibility for one's behavior is at the root of most definitions of mental health, not just adulthood. Various coping styles for dealing with life are termed neurotic if they allow people to avoid responsibility in one way or another, thereby preventing them from leading functional, adaptive lives. For the present, one such coping style is especially relevant to corporate life: obsessive-compulsive neurosis.

Many successful executives have risen to the top through extreme dedication, persistence, attention to detail, and perfectionism. These obsessive-compulsive traits are precisely what makes it so difficult for executives to commit to a completely integrated program of planned change. How are executives likely to deal with the anxiety that emanates from such an uncertain undertaking? They will insist on quick-fix approaches to organizational success.

One reason why executives are willing to spend so much time and money on one quick fix after another is that they know in their hearts that the quick fix will not change much of anything. The quick fix is the best way to avoid responsibility: It diverts the organization's energy while absolutely maintaining the status quo. Although no one will benefit from the quick fix, the important thing is that no one will get directly hurt either! The quick fix is relatively safe—and therefore perfect—from the point of view of an obsessive-compulsive executive.

The realization of the American dream rests on the promise of commitment. If senior executives do not act on this promise, the five tracks and all other efforts at providing multiple approaches will be wasted. Senior executives will continue to search for the Holy Grail, whether it be a magical machine to solve their business problems or a quick fix for their organizational problems. Continuing with such misplaced efforts eventually will reduce our productivity as a nation, threaten our standard of living and economic freedom, and erode our position of world leadership. The alternative is to tackle the fundamental problem facing our society today: failure to place long-term, total commitment behind an integrated program of planned organizational and institutional change.

## The Bottom Line

The six principles represent what is needed for managing dynamic complexity. One must recognize a holographic, three-dimensional view of the world. Such a worldview reveals complex problems that can be solved only by multiple approaches. Since a great diversity of expertise and information is needed to use multiple approaches effectively, participative management is the only way to bring forth the necessary knowledge *and* commitment for success. Further, this critical need for diverse information may very well transcend the conventional boundaries of the problem. Both internal and external consultants often are needed to do what the managers cannot or should not do on their own—collect sensitive information about management and organizational problems. Lastly, long-term organizational success cannot be achieved unless top management commits fully to a completely integrated program of planned change.

The six principles and their sharp distinctions will reappear throughout the remaining chapters of this book. The reader will be reminded of the complex hologram, complex problems, multiple approaches, participative management, consultants, and commitment. These elements are inescapable if we are serious about creating and maintaining organizational success. When the next era begins and the world is no longer complex, when problems are once again simple, when single approaches are sufficient for success, the tide may turn. Or a new dimension may be born, followed by a new image of the world.

# 2

# Understanding the Completely Integrated Program:

## The Critical Stages of Planned Change

> There is a religious side to American industry. It is forever seeking salvation, never sure what form the messiah will take.
> And just how does salvation manifest itself? Certainly not in the form of fads or gimmicks. We would certainly never put up with such nonsense! Salvation for American industry comes in the form of new or revised techniques, procedures, and methods to improve performance—"to impact the bottom line," as the current jargon would have it. Whatever ills exist, whatever weaknesses, the newest and latest will cure everything—particularly if it is imported from Japan. Last year it was Quality Circles; this year it is Zero Inventories.
> The truth is, one more panacea and we will all go nuts.
> —Gittler, 1985, p. 98

The field of organization development, as it first emerged in the 1950s, was envisioned as offering methods for systemwide change that would significantly improve the functioning of entire organizations. For the most part, however, this majestic vision has been lost and forgotten.

During the 1960s and 1970s, efforts at improving organizations became more and more specialized and, eventually, fragmented—primarily because they focused on the narrow use of single approaches, such as team building, survey feedback, and performance appraisal. Academics, following traditional guidelines for rigorous research, tended to develop improvement methods primarily suited for tightly controlled, isolated parts of the organization—thereby treating the organization as if it were a simple machine. Executives found this approach to be consistent with their own inclinations, of course, since it did not require them to examine either the open system or the holographic aspects of their organizations.

Today, however, as many organizations are coming to realize that "future shock" is upon them, the need for fundamental, systemwide changes is being voiced more and more frequently. Now entire organizations must be transformed into market-driven, innovative, and adaptive systems if they are to survive and prosper in the highly competitive, global environment of the next decades. Given this situation, there is an urgent need to rejuvenate the theory and practice of organization development—to supply programs for systemwide change.

## A Program of Planned Change

A completely integrated program for improving organizations must specify at least three elements: (1) all the controllable variables—via a complex hologram—that determine organizational success, (2) all the multiple approaches—consisting of techniques, instruments, and procedures—that can alter these controllable variables, and (3) all the ongoing activities—from beginning to end—that manage organization-wide change. *Organizational success* is a matter of creating and maintaining high performance and satisfaction for both internal and external stakeholders over an extended period of time.

Regarding the first ingredient, a completely integrated program must be guided by a holographic view of the barriers (problems) and channels (opportunities) that must be addressed if organizational success is to be achieved. It is essential that a complex hologram be used to pinpoint all these controllable variables—at the surface and below the surface—that can subsequently be used by managers and consultants as leverages for improving organizations.

Regarding the second ingredient, a completely integrated program must include multiple approaches for directly influencing the full range of leverage points that can *change* individual, group, and organizational behavior. As discussed in the previous chapter, a variety of techniques, instruments, and procedures for achieving organizational success can be organized into a sequence of five tracks: (1) the culture track, (2) the management skills track, (3) the team-building track, (4) the strategy-structure track, and (5) the reward system track. As a whole, these five tracks can alter all the controllable variables between the environment outside the organization and the psyche inside the individual.

Regarding the third ingredient, a completely integrated program must specify *how* systemwide change can be managed in an organization—given the complexities and dynamics of a living system. While the process of change can be managed by an arbitrary number of stages, phases, or steps (from the very beginning of the program to the end), I have found it useful to organize the "how" of planned change into five critical stages: (1) initiating the program, (2) diagnosing the problems, (3) scheduling the tracks, (4) implementing the tracks, and (5) evaluating the results. Only by viewing the organization holographically (the first ingredient) and surrounding the five tracks (the second ingredient) with the ongoing stages of planned change (the third ingredient) will continuous adaptability become ingrained in an organization—thereby managing beyond the quick fix.

Figure 2 shows the five stages of planned change as a recurring cycle of activity. To be successful, all programs for improving organizations must devote sufficient time and effort to complete each stage. Movement from one stage to the next, shown by the single arrows, should not take place until all the criteria for the earlier stages have been satisfied. Otherwise, any glossed-over stages will result in more difficulties later. Since most organizations have lagged far behind the dramatic changes that have taken place in their environment, they usually conduct major—transformational—change during the first cycle of the program. In subsequent cycles, organizations conduct mostly incremental—evolutionary—change, since they are then able to keep pace with dynamic complexity.

Figure 2. The Five Stages of Planned Change.

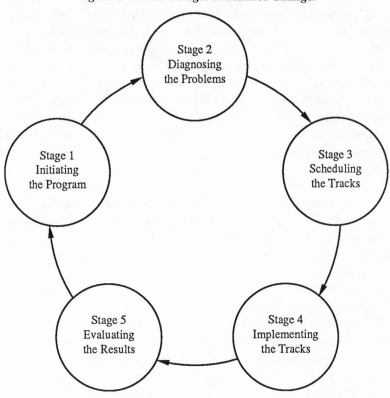

## Initiating the Program

I have found it useful to think of a window of opportunity for initiating planned change. This window opens somewhere between the point when an organization just begins to recognize its impending, systemwide problems and the point of crisis when members do not believe that the organization has the time and capacity to alter its gloomy prospects. Thus, some organizations are able to anticipate problems before a crisis arrives. This is the case when a number of senior executives agree that it might be easier to initiate planned change while the organization is still in a healthy state: Members might be more willing to participate in an improvement program when their jobs are not on the line and there are high expectations of long-term success. In most cases, however, an improvement program is initiated under difficult circumstances—sometimes, in fact, as a last resort. Seldom do managers and consultants come into partnership before the crunch.

The search for a program of planned change is often initiated informally by a few key executives of the firm. It begins when a manager is thrilled to learn that at least one other person also sees the systemwide problems facing the organization. After several discussions, they search out other managers or executives who either share their views or can be persuaded to see things the same, way. Eventually, when enough informal support of this kind has been mobilized, the executives find a way to put the topic of planned change (or whatever they choose to call it) on a meeting agenda. A discussion then ensues during which other executives learn about the issues and are given a chance to voice their opinions. If the necessary commitment has not been developed, the item will be dropped from the formal agenda and will once again become a topic for informal discussion among disgruntled managers. If the mobilization of commitment *has* been successful, however, a subcommittee will be formed to explore the question of large-scale change in much greater depth. Following a presentation of the subcommittee's deliberations, one or more executives are charged with the responsibility of leading the improvement effort.

The critical issue during "initiation" is whether the conditions exist for a successful improvement effort. Several key questions should be answered in the affirmative before the second stage—diagnosis—proceeds. The following questions pertain to the top executives of the whole organization and the senior executives of business units who are considering a major effort at organizational improvement.

*Do senior executives understand the concepts of complex holograms, complex problems, multiple approaches, participative management, consultants, and commitment?* As suggested in Chapter One, it would be unrealistic to expect executives to make a well-informed decision about whether to implement a completely integrated program of planned change if they do not have the concepts and the language to debate the key issues. It is crucial for the program's ultimate success that top executives know beforehand exactly what the program entails.

*Will the senior executives fully commit to implementing the whole program of planned change?* Once the executives know what to expect, the program's success requires their full commitment—in deed and not just in words. Sometimes, despite their commitment to follow through on the complete program, senior managers see the program as more relevant to the rest of the membership than to themselves. True commitment is evidenced when the senior executives openly acknowledge that they themselves are part of "the problem" and need to change as well. Such an admission sets the best example for the rest of the membership and encourages everyone to participate in a learning mode.

*Are the senior executives willing to have consultants diagnose the organization's full range of barriers to success?* While managers may believe they can conduct the diagnosis of problems themselves, this is the one area in which it is *imperative* to get an objective, independent reading of the organization's health. All the remaining stages of planned change rely on the diagnosis as *the* basis for choosing among various methods—techniques, instruments, and procedures—to bring about change and improvement. If the diagnosis is biased, inaccurate, or simplistic, the remaining stages of planned change will be jeopardized.

*Will the implementation of the improvement program be led by senior executives and will they take full responsibility for its success?* While most improvement efforts seem to be led by various staff groups—human resource, personnel, industrial relations, or employee relations—a completely integrated program for long-term organizational success should be led by line management, preferably by top management. With top management behind the change, the resources needed to conduct the whole program are more likely to be forthcoming. Moreover, with top management leading the charge, top priority will be assigned to the improvement effort in spite of all the pressures to concentrate on here-and-now business problems and operational issues. For example, if the organization is undergoing hard times—due to a recent crisis or financial setback— involvement in the program might take a back seat to other priorities. The program is most likely to be successful if it is presented by top management as *the* number one priority and is viewed as such by the rest of the membership.

## Diagnosing the Problems

When the key executives and consultants believe that all the conditions for success are present—that the program has been initiated properly—the diagnostic stage of planned change can proceed. Now the objective is to develop a deep understanding of the full range of problems (barriers) facing the organization as well as its opportunities (channels) for success.

Many organizations make use of various employee-opinion surveys to learn what members think about their jobs, their division, and the functioning of the whole organization. While the information gathered from such questionnaires is certainly systematic, I do not believe that any survey can uncover the true experience of life in a complex organization. Only a face-to-face discussion can hope to capture the full range of barriers to success— a holographic view. Even if it seems more efficient to interview groups of members instead of individuals one at a time, people will not voice their true feelings in front of other members unless the organization already has an open and trusting culture.

The consultants, with the aid of the managers, develop a plan to gather diagnostic information from members throughout the organization. The objective is to sample each level in the hierarchy—and each division and department—in order to get a representative view of the organization. Everyone in the top management group should be interviewed, simply because their views, and especially their commitment to change, are so critical to the program. If there are as many as 5,000 members in an organization, interviewing about 250 members should provide enough information to diagnose the organization's problems and opportunities. For smaller organizations or divisions, 50 to 150 interviews should be sufficient.

It is essential to be explicit about the model—the selective filter—that is used to ask questions and record responses during the interviews. If the interviewers see organizations only as interpersonal relationships, they will only ask questions and record responses with regard to interpersonal issues. The same holds true for seeing organizations as document-producing systems (strategies, organization charts, or job descriptions), as cultural phenomena, or in terms of management style. Any perceptual filter that hampers the search for a full understanding of the organization's problems will limit the variety of controllable variables—leverage points—that are considered and, subsequently, utilized.

Figure 3 shows organizational life as a complex hologram—a three-dimensional lens. This model is used for discovering the full range of barriers to success that can be transformed into channels for success. The model consists of five broad categories representing the at-the-surface (open system) aspects of an organization plus, at center stage, three below-the-surface aspects that add the dimension of depth. The five broad categories are the setting, the organization, the manager, the group, and the results. The three holographic aspects are culture, assumptions, and psyches. The double arrows

**Figure 3. The Barriers to Success Model.**

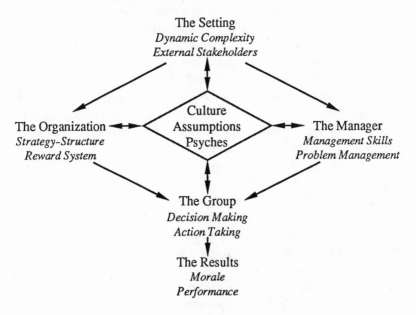

surrounding the "holographic diamond" signify the strong reciprocal influence between the three below-the-surface aspects and the other categories. Similarly, the single arrows show the primary (but not exclusive) impact that one category has on another. The model also shows how several categories combine to determine decision making and action taking, as well as morale and performance. Naturally, one could draw more double arrows showing how each aspect of the organization influences everything else; but there is no point served in further complicating a graphic representation of an already complex subject.

At the top of the Barriers to Success model is the broadest category of all: the setting. It includes every possible event and force that can affect the success of the organization. Any diagnosis that does not put the internal dynamics of the organization in context of its external setting is treating the organization as if it were a simple machine—not a living, breathing entity that is in a symbiotic relationship with its environment. Moreover, the history of the organization—when and how it was founded and the various environmental obstacles it has had to overcome since then—helps one to understand how the organization is likely to respond to the world today.

Two aspects of the setting deserve further discussion. The term *dynamic complexity*, introduced in Chapter One, summarizes the special qualities that are having an increasing impact on all organizations: rapid change and interdependence in a global marketplace. An *external stakeholder* is any individual, group, other organization, or community that has some stake in what the focal organization does—making dynamic complexity both unique and operational for every firm. Stakeholders vary according to the organization being studied. And new stakeholders can enter into the organization's setting at any time—for example, new competitors with improved products, new government agencies with new regulations, new research groups developing new production methods, and new consumers with different tastes. A critical diagnostic issue is whether the organization *anticipates* the actions of its external stakeholders or if it merely reacts to their initiatives.

On the left-hand side of the Barriers to Success model, the formal organization can be diagnosed according to its strategy-

structure and reward system. *Strategy* refers to all the documents
that signify direction: statements of vision, mission, purpose, goals,
and objectives. *Structure* refers to the way resources are organized
into action: organization charts, policy statements, job descriptions,
formal rules and regulations, and work procedures. The *reward
system* includes all documented methods to attract and retain
employees and, in particular, to motivate them to high levels of
performance. The essential diagnostic issue is whether all these
documented systems are barriers (or channels) to success: Is there too
much bureaucratic red tape that strangles creative, innovative, and
discretionary behavior? Are members asking for more clarity about
their objectives and for more guidelines on how to perform their
tasks?

On the right-hand side of the Barriers to Success model, the
managers can be diagnosed according to how well their styles and
skills fit with the types of people and problems in the organization.
Until recently, managers have been thought of primarily as decision
makers—persons who must choose from a set of alternatives to
arrive at an optimal or satisfactory solution. This is all well and
good if the alternatives are already determined and the rules for
choosing among them are clear-cut. In a setting of dynamic
complexity, however, it may not even be clear what the essential
problem is, let alone what the alternative choices are. Today's
managers need to be problem managers, who must sense and define
problems before they select and implement solutions. The critical
diagnostic issue here is whether managers throughout the organization are applying the right skills for addressing complex problems.

At the center of the Barriers to Success model, the uniquely
holographic, below-the-surface aspects of the organization can be
diagnosed: culture, assumptions, and psyches. Each of these aspects
functions at a different level of depth.

Just below the surface, and thus easiest of the three to
manage, is culture: the invisible force behind the tangibles and
observables in an organization, the social energy that moves the
membership into action. Culture is defined as *shared* values, beliefs,
expectations, and norms. Norms are easiest to define. They are the
unwritten rules of the game: Don't disagree with your boss; don't
rock the boat; don't share information with other groups. These

norms are seldom written or discussed. Often, work groups pressure their members to follow such dysfunctional norms out of habit. One consequence of this pressure is that culture—as manifested in norms of behavior—greatly affects how formal statements get interpreted and provides what written documents leave out. The fundamental diagnostic question, therefore, is this: Does the culture support the behavior that is needed for organizational success today (or does it pressure members to live according to what worked yesterday)?

The second holographic aspect of organizations—assumptions—is found at the next level of depth. Simply put, assumptions are beliefs whose truth has been taken for granted but that may turn out to be false under closer analysis. Underlying every decision and every action is a vast set of generally unstated and untested assumptions. Managers may well assume that the following unstated beliefs are unquestionably true: No new competitors will enter the industry; the economy will steadily improve; the consumer will buy whatever the firm produces; employees will continue to accept the same working conditions. The key diagnostic question to be asked is whether the critical assumptions that affect all major business decisions are up to date, explicit, understood, and utilized by members throughout the organization.

The third holographic aspect of organizations is also the deepest: the innermost qualities of the human mind and spirit. While psyches cannot be changed in a short period of time, if at all, an accurate understanding of human nature is essential in order to manage organizations and solve problems. In essence, the assumptions that members make concerning human nature—what people want, fear, resist, support, and defend—underlie the eventual success or failure of every decision and action. A useful diagnostic question is whether managers are frequently surprised when their proposed solutions are not accepted by their subordinates—suggesting inaccurate assumptions about some aspect of human behavior.

The lower part of the Barriers to Success model portrays the central role that groups must play in organizational decision making and action taking—and indicates the close link between the group and the results: performance and morale from the point of view of internal stakeholders. While individuals do act on their own volition, today's organization requires multiple contributions from members of one or more groups in order to manage complex problems. It is the synergistic team approach that will result in high-quality decisions *and* members' commitment to implement these decisions for organizational success.

The complex hologram for diagnosing organizations illustrates why the team approach will fail in most organizations where all the other barriers to success are still in place. If a manager does not use the proper styles and skills to manage complex problems, group decisions will be made by majority rule or by the dictates of the manager herself. If the culture pressures members to withhold information so that everyone can protect his or her own turf, the quality of decisions will again be adversely affected. If the organization's strategy is rooted in false assumptions about the consumer and the firm's competitors, every group decision will be moving the organization in the wrong direction. If the organization's structure makes it difficult for members in different departments to meet and discuss important issues, the group will simply lack the expertise and information needed to make high-quality decisions. Furthermore, if the reward system encourages individual versus team efforts, members will not be motivated to commit themselves to the group decision-making process in the first place. Indeed, only if an organization is composed of well-functioning teams, with negligible barriers to success in every category, can it become a truly breakaway company in a competitive world.

These interrelated dynamics, as captured by the Barriers to Success model, illustrate the variety of issues that arise again and again while diagnosing organizations. Naturally, there are differences from one organization to another and from one nation to another; there is always some unique circumstance or history that moderates the extent and variety of these basic issues. Nevertheless, I must emphasize the uncanny pattern that has emerged in all the work I have done in organizations: Rarely do I find that the formal organization *alone* needs readjustment for organizational success. Rarely do I find that managers' learning of new skills about complex problems will *by itself* solve the organization's performance and morale problems. I have never encountered a case in any nation in the world in which only the culture lagged behind and there was an effective formal organization already in place with managers applying up-to-date skills. The culture problem has *always* been associated with problems in the organization, the group, and the manager as well.

These general findings are not really surprising. Seeing the organization as a holographic image reveals an interrelated set of above-the-surface and below-the-surface problems and opportunities. Given such a perspective, what is the likelihood that today's organizations can cope with dynamic complexity and shifting stakeholders by adjusting only one category in the Barriers to Success model? It is very unlikely indeed. But what about adjusting most but not all the categories shown in the holographic model? That is just as unlikely to be successful, sorry to say. Rather, it seems that *every* category has to be considered and dealt with in all cases. This is the new rule for creating and maintaining organizational success, not the exception. Adjustments in culture, skills, groups, strategies, structures, and reward systems, all undertaken with an enlightened view of the world and its various stakeholders, are necessary to achieve the results our organizations desire.

Once all the interviews have been conducted, the consultants organize the variety of problems they have discovered by sorting them into the categories of the Barriers to Success model. Then they propose how a specially tailored, five-track program can remove all the barriers to success—by building on the channels to success (the positive aspects of the organization that should be retained). A report is prepared and presented first to the top managers. Although these top managers may have accepted the fact that their problems required help, they may not have sensed their seriousness and extent. Often surprise and shock follow the formal presentation, and much more discussion is needed before the top managers can move forward. There may even be strong defensive reactions— denying or minimizing what has been reported. Some of this defensiveness is quite natural, since the managers are no doubt feeling guilty for being part of the problem. If their egos are bruised, it will take some time for them to move from the defensive stage to the acceptance phase. This process can take a few days or even a few months. The consultants can help by articulating these normal human reactions and by indicating how managers in other organizations have struggled with the same feelings. Sometimes these open discussions about hurt egos take an incredible burden off the top managers, who have come to see themselves as all-knowing, all-powerful, and, therefore, all-responsible for anything and everything that happens to their organization. As their human nature is affirmed, it becomes easier to get on with addressing the organization's problems—and opportunities.

When the top managers have accepted the general diagnosis, it is time to discuss these findings with the entire membership. Naturally, it takes conviction for the top managers to be willing to present the diagnosis to others. But this willingness is critical, for it demonstrates commitment to the membership. Top managers acknowledging problems to themselves and to others, while painful, is a crucial event in the life of an organization: it promotes credibility, confidence, and action.

### Scheduling the Tracks

The next stage of planned change—scheduling the tracks—involves (1) selecting the first unit to participate in the program and planning the spread of change to the remaining units, (2) selecting the techniques (methods for bringing about change) that will make up each of the five tracks in each unit in order to address the problems identified during the diagnostic stage, and (3) scheduling the five tracks into a timed sequence of activity in order to promote effective learning and change in each organizational unit. Once a plan for action has been formalized, managers, members, and consultants will work together to apply it in the next stage: implementing the tracks.

Scheduling the five tracks first requires a decision as to which unit of the organization should begin the program. Sometimes an autonomous business unit is chosen for a pilot project; other times, corporate headquarters might be the first unit scheduled for the program. Following an evaluation of the results (the final stage of planned change), other business units proceed to implement the whole improvement effort. This schedule continues until all business units desiring or requiring change have implemented some version of the five tracks.

My experience in scheduling units for planned change

suggests that the first business unit chosen should be a *primary* business unit. Why? The answer is credibility. Which unit would serve as the best example to other units that planned change is not only important but possible? In most cases, I have found that the business units selected for planned change are isolated from the core business of the organization. Perhaps this represents a safe strategy: If the program fails, the whole organization is hardly affected. If the program *is* successful, however, the other business units will not regard the pilot project as a relevant example of what they should be doing. If the intent is to spread change throughout the organization, units should be chosen that are critical to the success of the whole enterprise—even though this necessarily involves greater risk. This risk, however, should be reason enough for top executives to do whatever it takes to make the program a success.

A plan is then developed that specifies the ways in which change can be spread throughout the organization. This plan outlines not only the order in which the remaining units will be scheduled but also the supporting techniques and procedures that will be used once the pilot project is under way (and as other units begin the process)—for example, the rest of the organization can be kept informed of what is taking place and why. Some managers or members from the pilot project might be temporarily transferred to the next unit to help facilitate the changes. Moreover, various rewards and perquisites might be offered to units participating in the program in order to convey its importance.

The choice of the pilot project and the sequence and methods by which other business units participate certainly vary from company to company. What makes each application of the program different are the techniques used in each of the five tracks. Just as the diagnosis varies for each organizational unit, so does the choice of technique to address each problem. In some cases the management skills track will include material on leadership styles, conflict-handling modes, and ways of minimizing defensive communication. If the managers have already acquired these skills, management training moves directly to teaching methods for managing complex problems. Clearly, managers and consultants should be aware of the diversity of techniques that exist so they can choose the ones that best fit the problems in each organizational unit.

The five tracks, in all cases, are scheduled in the prescribed order. The first three tracks (culture, management skills, and team-building) adjust the behavioral infrastructure of the organization—the blood and guts of how people behave toward one another on the job. The last two tracks (strategy-structure and reward system) adjust the organization's tangible features—the documents, technologies, systems, and resources that guide people's behavior toward an agreed-upon mission. Without first developing an adaptive *inner* organization, any adjustments to the outer organization would be cosmetic and, therefore, short-lived.

The culture track is the best place to commence the process of change: It serves as the icebreaker to encourage introspection and a willingness to change. Members enjoy—even laugh at—the revelations that occur as the dysfunctional norms—the unwritten rules of the game—are brought to everyone's attention. It is also much easier to blame norms than to blame oneself or other people. As long as members take responsibility for change, it does not really matter if they use norms as a scapegoat to take some of the pressure off their egos. Usually, in the first few sessions of the culture track, members begin having more relaxed conversations within and between work groups, begin sharing more work-related matters among themselves, and begin believing that something very different is happening in the organization.

Once managers become receptive to change—through the culture track—they can be taught the full set of skills needed to conduct effective problem management for today's complex world. And, given that the culture is encouraging more trust and openness, members now can learn how to analyze their previously unstated assumptions before any critical decisions are made.

After the first two tracks have given the members some valuable classroom instruction on culture and skills, the next effort lies in applying what has been learned to the organization. The team-building track is designed to transfer the new cultural norms and management skills into the everyday activities of each work group. Once each work group can address its complex problems effectively on its own, the team-building track then focuses on intergroup and interdepartmental relations—to foster cooperative efforts *across* group boundaries. In this way, all available expertise and information can be marshaled to manage the complex technical and business problems that arise within and between work groups.

Eventually it becomes time for the membership to take on one of the toughest problems facing any organization in a dynamic environment: aligning its formally documented systems. One might think that the firm's mission and its corresponding strategic choices should have been the first topics addressed. Is it not logical to find out the direction in which the organization wants to go before the rest of the system is put in place? Logical, yes. But there are other forces operating in a complex organization besides logic. Understanding the impact of culture, assumptions, and psyches—the third dimension of the complex hologram—leads to several conclusions: It makes little sense to plan the future direction of the firm if members do not trust one another and refuse to share crucial information with one another, expose their tried and true assumptions, or commit themselves to the new direction. If the prior tracks have not accomplished their purposes, the strategy-structure problem will be addressed through political maneuvering by vested interests—not through an open exchange of ideas and a cooperative effort to achieve organizational success.

Once the organization is moving in the right direction with the properly aligned structure, the reward system track completes the first cycle of the improvement program by paying for performance. Just as in the case of the strategy-structure track, however, the reward system track is futile if all the other tracks have not been managed properly. Without a supportive culture, members will not believe that rewards are tied to performance—regardless of what the formal documents state. Instead, they will believe it is useless to work hard since they think rewards are based on favoritism and politics. Similarly, if managers do not have the skills needed to appraise performance, no reward system, no matter how well intentioned, can succeed. A poor appraisal will cause defensiveness, which will inhibit each member's motivation to improve his or her performance. Without effective teams, managers and members will be reluctant to discuss—face to face—the results of performance reviews and the distribution of rewards. And in the absence of such discussion, imaginations will run wild, since nobody will know for sure whether high performers receive significantly more rewards ₜhan low performers. Furthermore, if the strategy and structure are not designed properly, the reward system cannot measure performance objectively. Only if each group is autonomous can its output be assessed as a separate quantity as close to the individual level as possible. The latter condition is essential to make the pay-for-performance link a reality in everyone's eyes.

Figure 4 illustrates the scheduling of the five tracks—as an example only, since each case is different. The horizontal line for each track signifies an ongoing series of off-site meetings (in a workshop environment) and on-site meetings (organized at the workplace) set up to pursue the topic in question (for example, cultural change). As the figure shows, a track does not have to be completed before the next track is initiated. The guiding principle is that the earlier track should have established the conditions necessary for the next track to succeed. A new approach to problems can take place in each work group, for example, before the desired culture change is complete and all new skills have been learned.

**Figure 4. Scheduling the Five Tracks.**

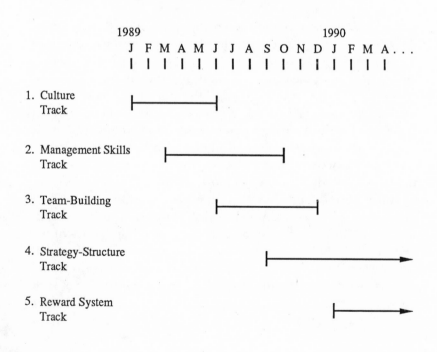

Similarly, members who will be participating in either the strategy-structure or the reward system tracks can begin their discussions before each work group is an effective team.

Scheduling the five tracks also requires numerous choices regarding personnel. Who will be involved in each track? Typically, the culture track includes every work group in the organization (or business unit). As we will see, ensuring every member's involvement in workshop sessions is the only way to change something as ingrained as corporate culture. Since, in most cases, an open and trusting culture will not be evident in the organization for several months to come (at least not until the team-building track is initiated), every work group is subdivided into peer groups for each workshop in the culture track. In virtually all cases, these peer groups are formed by separating superiors from their subordinates, since these subgroups provide the best opportunity for a candid and forthright conversation. (Peer groups, however, can also be formed according to other criteria—*any* status distinction, for example— that will foster a safe environment for learning and change.)

Scheduling the management skills track usually involves all the managers in the organization (or designated business units)— from first-line supervisors through the chief executive officer. Sometimes, key professional personnel and potential managers are included for purposes of career development. Just as in the culture track, however, all group discussions take place in peer groups—to foster open communication before the culture has changed.

Scheduling the team-building track brings the superiors back together with their subordinates in their formal organizational units. This is the only way to ensure that the new knowledge gained from the workshop sessions can be transferred directly to the job. If, however, the superiors and subordinates are brought together too early, before the new culture and skills have been internalized, almost everyone will fall back to business as usual. It does take some time—in a relatively safe environment—for people to learn new behavior and skills *before* they can approach emotionally charged situations in new ways.

Scheduling the last two tracks generally involves the formation of two separate task forces of about twenty-five persons each. One task force addresses the strategy-structure problems that were revealed during the diagnostic stage while the other task force addresses the reward system problems. The people chosen for these special missions not only represent all levels and areas in the company, but they also have demonstrated leadership during the prior tracks of the program. Following their deliberations, these two task forces present their recommendations to top management for improving the organization's strategy-structure and reward system. Subsequently, these groups play a key role in helping to implement the recommended changes.

If the program of planned change is scheduled over too long a period of time, the membership will gradually lose interest and become disillusioned because the promised benefits, such as a well-functioning reward system, do not materialize. If the program is scheduled for too short a time period, however, it will be impossible to lay the foundation for the successful completion of each track, and the membership will experience difficulties or even failure as the program proceeds. How often, then, should the various workshop activities be scheduled for the participants in the program? The best answer is somewhere between every other week and every other month, in most cases.

### Implementing the Tracks

It is one thing to schedule the five tracks, but it is quite another to adjust the schedule as it is being implemented. The plan *never* takes place exactly as intended. There are always surprises. Human nature and human systems do not lend themselves to an entirely predictable path. Besides, if people feel they are being programmed in any way, it is not unlike them to purposely do something illogical, irrational, or unexpected just to show how independent they really are.

The key issue throughout implementation, therefore, is flexibility. As the schedule is implemented, the managers and consultants must look for cues, take suggestions, and, in short, adapt. For example, special requests will be made for counseling sessions, feedback sessions for staff meetings, additional culture sessions, more management skills training, and so forth. In each case, managers and consultants must consider the request and respond according to their principles and their sense of what will work. Sometimes requests may be turned down, but the reasons should always be stated. At other times, the requests may be acted upon—but in a fashion different from that first suggested. Often it is the managers themselves who initiate additional activity, adjusting to what they perceive is needed—to nudge this person or that group or to support some effort that turned out to be tougher than anticipated.

The detailed theories and methods for implementing each of the five tracks in a flexible, adaptive manner are provided in the next five chapters. The following discussion, therefore, only presents some general approaches for managing the implementation process, including some typical experiences and time frames.

A "shadow" track (running parallel to all the five tracks) is recommended to ensure the successful implementation of the program; this track places primary responsibility for the program on the shoulders of the "shadow" group. This group of approximately ten to fifteen members, mostly senior executives but also members representing other levels and areas in the organization, meets regularly to monitor the program and discover ways of improving the whole process of implementation. This shadow group might monitor every written document distributed by the executive office, for example, to ensure that a consistent signal is being sent. If the content or tone of a memo on a new policy seems deficient or out of key, the shadow group reviews it and suggests how it could be reworded to agree with the program's intent. In essence, the shadow group is encouraged to be as imaginative as possible in making sure that the program succeeds.

The most enjoyable part of the implementation stage is seeing changes and improvements take hold. Initially, everyone is a little leery of what to expect and unsure whether the organization has the ability to change. As early successes are won, however, confidence develops, and this inspires an even greater effort at improvement. This is not to suggest that the road will be smooth and without obstacles. Week by week, some things will get a lot worse before they get better. When an event seems to reinforce the old ways or attitudes of the past, it is easy to be discouraged and feel that nothing has changed. But if instead of examining week-by-week fluctuations one looks at month-by-month trends, the process will probably show a definite pattern of improvement.

These fluctuations in perceived accomplishments and moods illustrate the importance of setting realistic expectations in the beginning—what should happen and when—and making sure that impatience does not raise members' expectations to unattainable levels. Disappointment and frustration result when expectations are out of line with reality, which subsequently affects both the individual's and the organization's confidence to continue the program. Expectations must be managed very carefully throughout the program of planned change, particularly by the shadow track.

A fundamental issue that always arises during implementation is whether members will take personal responsibility for change. Even after having participated in several workshops on culture and management skills, members keep waiting for something to happen: "My boss still doesn't keep me informed of what goes on." "The other groups still don't cooperate with us." "My subordinates still don't complete their work on time." "When will this organization change?"

Rotter's (1971) distinction between internal and external control is exceedingly useful in challenging members to look at themselves rather than point the finger at others. *External control* is when a person believes that what happens to him is determined by outside forces (luck, politics, other people's behavior). *Internal control* is when a person believes that what happens to him is determined by what he does (his own decisions, attitudes, behavior). Naturally, internal control helps people take responsibility for change; external control shifts all the attention to someone else.

Who *is* the source of organizational change? Discussions of this question, usually during the first two tracks of the program, translate into action when they are supplemented by this exercise: First, each member lists the things he has done differently since the improvement program began. Then each member shares his list with the rest of the work group members. Next each member asks his associates if they have witnessed what he claims. If they have not observed these changes, the member must be prepared to act on his good intentions—to demonstrate internal control and personal responsibility for change. Gradually, members begin to talk about their experiences in a very different way from before: "I've convinced my boss that I can do a better job if I know more about her priorities." "I've spent more time getting to know the people in other departments." "I now tell my subordinates the reasons why I need something done on a given date." "This organization is really changing!"

After a number of months go by, it will become more and more apparent that the membership has internalized the desired behavior. Now the new ways are enacted quite automatically as the new behavior becomes easier to put into everyday practice. At a certain point—typically sometime during the team-building track when the new culture and skills become internalized—the hump is crossed and the old gives way to the new. The best way I can describe this transition is to say that members could not return to the old ways even if they tried to, because the new ways are so obviously better and contribute more to personal satisfaction *and* organizational success.

How long will the process of implementation take? One can expect the first cycle of implementing all five tracks to take anywhere from one to five years. A period of less than one year might work for a small division in which the barriers to success are minimal. A program taking more than five years might be necessary for a large, older organization that must break with its past in practically every way. If the program were to take more than ten years, I would assume there was insufficient commitment over this time period—and hence no momentum for change to prevail.

### Evaluating the Results

There are essentially three reasons for evaluating the results of the program. The first purpose involves collecting information during the pilot project (or any earlier application of the five tracks) in order to improve the implementation process for the remaining units. The shadow group should keep a close watch on the pilot project so that new insights and methods can be adopted as one unit after another embarks on the path of planned change.

The second purpose for evaluation recognizes that planned change is never complete—it is ongoing and forever. Thus the results of every application are evaluated to discover barriers that still need attention. An evaluation might reveal, for example, the need to improve the culture in a few of the more troublesome work groups. Or, if new managers enter an organizational unit after most of the program has been implemented, additional skills-training sessions can be conducted to bring the new managers up to speed with the rest of the membership. Typically, cycling through the stages of planned change a second or third time, as guided by the evaluation stage, entails fine tuning (incremental change) rather than corporate transformation (revolutionary change).

Both the first and second purposes for evaluation (collecting information in the pilot project in order to benefit other organizational units and collecting information to help each unit itself remove its remaining barriers to success) can be accomplished by engaging in another round of face-to-face interviews. If diagnostic interviews were the most effective way to learn about the organization's barriers (and channels) at the beginning of the program, the same approach can be applied again to assess what could have been done differently and to discover what still needs to be done in order to remove any remaining barriers to success. I find it useful to have internal consultants conduct these evaluation interviews rather than the external consultants who conducted the diagnostic interviews.

The third purpose for evaluation is to determine whether the program has achieved the intended results: improved organizational success. From the viewpoint of stakeholders—consumers, stockholders, suppliers, federal agencies, the community—one usually can suggest some "hard" outcome measures: return on investment, earnings per share, profit, sales, number of clients served, market share, budget increases, number of patents and new products, new contracts and orders, productivity gains, and so on. Making a before-and-after comparison on any of these measures (before and after the improvement effort) should provide a solid basis for assessing the program's impact. If the whole endeavor was successful, the differences in these measures should be evident—or so the argument goes.

While these bottom-line measures certainly can be convincing, one has to recognize their limitations. One should not overlook the time lag between decisions and actions on the one hand and performance on the other. Some of the bottom-line measures will not be affected until months or years after a key decision has been made. Improved decision making that results in new approaches to product development will not be felt in the organization's setting for years, for example. If the before-and-after comparisons are made right after the improvement program has concluded, one cannot expect external stakeholders to notice any observable differences. Ironically, if such before-and-after comparisons were to suggest significant improvements (or declines), they probably would be spurious. Only if these measurements are made over a long enough period of time—a period in which *true* effects can be expected—can one take the results of such an "objective" evaluation seriously.

## The Bottom Line

While the five stages of planned change are certainly complex, so are the problems that this program is designed to resolve. A completely integrated program must be able to affect every controllable variable in the organization, not just one or two. At the same time, if the whole program is not initiated properly with top management's support and if the organization's problems are not diagnosed correctly, the program cannot produce its potential benefits. Moreover, the program's implementation must be *integrated* and *flexible*. Attempting to quick fix a program for planned change would do the organizational sciences—and the organization in question—a great disservice.

# 3

# The Culture Track:

## Establishing Trust, Information Sharing, and Adaptiveness

Social forces are transforming our groups. Cultural norms develop, teaching us what is expected, supported, and accepted by the people we live and work with. These norms exert powerful pressure, causing us to behave in ways that often run counter to our real wishes and goals.

As individuals we are almost all affected. How many of us, at one time or another, have joined a group or organization with the intention of working to change some of the things that seemed to be wrong with group behavior? And how many of us have found ourselves five to ten years later fully involved in the same behavior that we had once rejected?

—Allen, 1980, pp. 31-32

The likelihood that an organization will achieve success in a dynamic and complex setting is not determined just by the skills of its leaders. Nor will its adaptiveness be primarily determined by the strategy-structure and reward system that make up its visible features. Rather, every organization has an invisible quality—a certain style, a character, a way of doing things—that ultimately determines whether success will be achieved. Ironically, what cannot be seen or touched may be more powerful than the dictates of any one person or any formally documented system. To understand the soul of the organization, therefore, requires that we travel below

the charts, rulebooks, machines, and buildings into the underground world of corporate culture.

Culture is the invisible force behind the tangibles and
observables in an organization, a social energy that moves the
people into action. Culture is to the organization what personality
is to the individual—a hidden yet unifying theme that provides
meaning, direction, and mobilization. A person has to experience
the social energy that flows from shared commitments among
group members to know it: the energy that emanates from mutual
influence, "one for all and all for one," and "esprit de corps."

An *adaptive* culture is evident when members actively
support one another's efforts to identify all the problems and
implement workable solutions. There is a feeling of confidence:
The members believe, without a doubt, that they can manage
whatever new problems and opportunities come their way. There is
a widespread enthusiasm, a spirit of doing whatever it takes to
achieve organizational success. The members are receptive to
change.

A *dysfunctional* culture is evident when the social energy of
the organization steers members in the wrong direction: Work
groups pressure their members to persist in behavior that may have
worked well in the past but is clearly inappropriate today. Gradually, the organization falls into a *culture rut*—members pursue
things blindly and unconsciously out of habit. There is no
adaptation or change; routine motions are made again and again,
even though success is not forthcoming. Here the social energy not
only works against the organization but is contrary to the members'
private wishes. Nobody wants to be ineffective and dissatisfied, but
everyone pressures one another to comply with the unstated, below-
the-surface, behind-the-scenes, invisible culture. Even though
morale and performance suffer, this rut can go on for years. Bad
habits die hard.

Eventually, a dysfunctional culture may lead to a collective
depression in which the organization's social energy becomes
deactivated: It is not mobilized toward anything. Most members
seem listless about their jobs. They no longer pressure one another
to do anything. Pronouncements by top managers promising to
improve the situation fall on deaf ears. The members have heard

these promises before. Nothing seems to matter. The soul of the organization is slowly dying.

*Culture shock* occurs when the sleeping organization awakes to find that it has lost touch with its mission, its setting, and its assumptions. The new world has left the insulated company behind. Rather than experience this shock, the organization may decide not to wake up. Its managers simply continue to believe in the myth of erroneous extrapolation: What made the organization successful in the past will make it successful in the future.

The first part of this chapter explores two interrelated questions: How do cultures form—what brings them into being? And how do cultures persist—what forces keep them intact? Understanding the answers to these questions is essential for managing cultures. In these discussions, we will see how norms— rather than any other manifestation of culture—provide the leverage points for managing the five steps of the culture track: (1) surfacing actual norms, (2) establishing desired norms, (3) identifying culture-gaps, (4) closing culture-gaps, and (5) sustaining cultural change. Implementing these steps provides the foundation for all other improvement efforts, including the remaining four tracks of the program.

### How Do Cultures Form?

A culture often forms quickly in response to the organization's mission, its setting, and what is required for success: quality, efficiency, product reliability, customer service, innovation, hard work, loyalty. When the organization is born, a tremendous energy is released as members struggle to make the company work. The culture reflects everyone's drive and imagination. As the reward system and rules governing work are formally documented, they begin to shape the initial culture, suggesting what behavior and attitudes are important for success.

Such forces in shaping culture are further heightened by the impact of key individuals. The founder's objectives, principles, values, and behavior, for example, provide important clues as to what is expected from all members both now and in the future. Other top executives follow the founder's lead and pass on the company culture to their subordinates. Edson W. Spencer, chief executive officer and chairman of Honeywell, Inc., realizes the impact he has had on corporate culture ("Conversation . . . ," 1983, p. 43):

> Most of us, very humbly, don't wish to acknowledge that fact, but nonetheless the chief executive's tone, his integrity, his standards, his way of dealing with people, his focusing on things that are important or not important can have a profound impact on the rest of the organization. What I am saying is that the way the chief executive and senior managers of the company conduct themselves as individuals has a more profound impact on how other people in the company conduct *themselves* than anything else that happens.

Employees also take note of all critical incidents that stem from management's actions—such as the time so-and-so was reprimanded for doing a good job just because she was not asked to do it beforehand. Such incidents become the folklore that people remember, indicating what the corporation really wants, what really counts in getting ahead, or, alternatively, how to stay out of trouble. Work groups adopt these lessons as *norms* on how to survive, how to protect oneself from the system, and how to retaliate against the organization for its past transgressions. Lewicki (1981, pp. 8-9) suggests how the double standard—managers asking for one type of behavior while rewarding another—motivates employees to develop unwritten rules to survive and prosper:

> What an organization says it expects should be consistent with what it rewards—but that's not always so. If an organization says it wants to aggressively develop new businesses, then presumably it should reward those who are the most aggressive in new business development. However, if it consistently promotes those who have done the best job in nurturing current accounts and ignores the entrepreneurs, employees will soon get the message that an organiza-

tional double standard exists. Employee discontent about this duplicity will soon find its way into lunch table or cocktail circuit conversation, where the "do's and don'ts" of organizational life are shared, evaluated, and communicated to new members. "Don't listen to what management says," oldtimers will warn; "do what others have been rewarded for."

As a culture forms around a recognized need, a setting, and specific task requirements, it may be very functional at first. But in time the culture becomes an entity unto itself, independent of the initial reasons and critical incidents that formed it. As long as it supports the organization's mission, the culture remains in the background. But if management attempts to make significant changes that have an impact on everyone's behavior, the culture rises to the occasion.

The hidden power of the culture is apparent when management attempts to make a major strategic shift or tries to adopt entirely new work methods. Management cannot pinpoint the source of apathy, resistance, or rebellion and wonders why the new work methods are not automatically and enthusiastically embraced by the membership. To management, it is obvious that these proposed changes are necessary and desirable. Why cannot everyone else see this? The reason is that the changes run counter to the culture that underlies the organization.

Top management is also caught in the grip of the firm's separate and distinct culture. Employees from below wonder why managers "play it so safe" and why they keep applying the same authoritarian styles even though they simply do not work. Employees wonder why management is so blind to the world around them. They wonder if management is mean or just plain stupid.

### How Do Cultures Persist?

Cultural norms become embedded in the organization when group members agree on what constitutes appropriate behavior. If a norm is violated—if someone behaves differently from what the norm dictates—there are immediate and strong pressures to get the offending party to change her behavior. For example, one norm in a company might be: Don't disagree with your boss in public. Consider a person who insists on presenting her reservations about the company's new product at a group meeting just after her boss has argued for making a large investment in the advertising campaign. The critic is stared at, frowned at, looked at with rolling eyes, and given other nonverbal messages to shut up and sit down. If these efforts do not silence her, she will hear about it later, either from her coworkers or from her boss.

A simple experiment conducted by Asch (1955) demonstrates just how powerfully the group can influence its members' behavior. The experiment was presented to subjects as a study in perceptions. Three lines—A, B, and C, all of different lengths—were shown on a single card. Subjects were asked to indicate which of these three lines was identical in length to a fourth line, D, shown on a second card. Seven persons sat in a row. One by one they indicated their choices. Although line D was in fact identical to line C, each of the first six persons, confederates of the experimenter, said that line D was identical to A. The seventh person was the unknowing subject. As the six confederates each gave the agreed-upon incorrect response, the true subject usually became increasingly uneasy, anxious, and doubtful of his or her own perceptions. Subjects agreed with the six confederates about 40 percent of the time. When no other people were present, subjects chose the wrong line less than 1 percent of the time.

In this experiment, which has been duplicated many times, there was no opportunity for the seven subjects to discuss the problem among themselves. If there had been such an opportunity, the effect would have been stronger, because the six confederates would attempt to influence the seventh person. It is not easy being a deviant in a group when everyone else is against you. Every person's need to be accepted by a group—family, friends, coworkers, or neighbors—gives a group leverage to demand compliance with its norms. If people did not care about acceptance at all, a group would have little hold, other than formal sanctions, over individuals. Most people, therefore, will deny their own perceptions when confronted with the group's norms of "objective" reality. Objective reality thus becomes a *social* reality.

Imagine just how easily such socially defined (and distorted) perceptions of reality can persist when backed by formal sanctions such as pay, promotions, and other rewards. The group or the entire organization can reward its members so that they ignore not only the changes taking place in the environment but also the disruptive behavior of troublemakers inside the organization. The members collectively believe that everything is fine, and they continue to reinforce this myth and reward one another for maintaining it. In essence, everyone agrees that the dysfunctional ways can continue without question. Any deviant who thinks otherwise is severely punished and eventually banished from the tribe.

## Managing Cultural Norms

Why does one organization have a very adaptive culture while another's culture lives in the past? Is one a case of good fortune and the other a result of bad luck? On the contrary, it seems that any organization can find itself with an outdated culture if its culture is not managed explicitly.

If left alone, all cultures eventually become dysfunctional. Fear, insecurity, oversensitivity, dependency, and paranoia seem to take over unless a concerted effort to establish an adaptive culture is undertaken. Everyone has been hurt at one time or another in his or her life, particularly in childhood. It is, therefore, rather easy to scare people into worrying about what pain will be inflicted in the future, even in a relatively nonthreatening situation. As a result, people cope by protecting themselves, by being cautious, by minimizing their risks, by going along with a culture that builds protective barriers around work units and around the whole organization.

If we understand how cultures first form and then persist, we can prevent them from becoming dysfunctional. With the steps of the culture track—reinforced by the remaining four tracks—we can transform a long-standing dysfunctional culture into an adaptive one. Although culture manifests itself through stories, rituals, symbols, slogans, and songs, the way to redirect dysfunctional organizational behavior is by managing norms. Even norms that dictate how one should behave, the opinions one should state, and one's facial expressions can be surfaced, discussed, and altered.

### Step One: Surfacing Actual Norms

In a workshop setting without any superiors present, the first step in the culture track is for all group members to list the norms that currently guide their behavior and attitudes. To get the process started, sometimes it helps to remind group members of the current "do's and don't's" of behavior, as summarized in the culture section of the diagnostic report that was provided to the membership (see Chapter Two). Other times it takes a little prodding and a few illustrations to get the discussion going, but once it begins members are quick to suggest many norms. In fact, they seem to delight in being able to articulate what was never stated in any document and rarely mentioned in conversation.

When an organization's culture is dysfunctional, people may list norms like these: Look busy even when you're not; don't be the first to disagree; don't step on the toes of senior management; laugh at those who suggest new ways of doing things; complain a lot; don't be the bearer of bad news; shoot the messenger who brings bad news; don't trust anyone who seems sincere; ridicule the work of other groups. Ironically, the one norm that must be violated so that this list can be developed is: Don't make norms explicit!

### Step Two: Establishing Desired Norms

The second step in the culture track is for all group members to list the norms that would lead to organizational success. At this point, the members usually recognize the impact that unwritten rules have had on their behavior. They feel a sense of relief as a new way of life is considered. They realize that they no longer have to pressure one another to behave in dysfunctional ways. The members can create a new social order within their own work groups and within their own organization. Part of this sense of relief comes from recognizing that their dissatisfactions and ineffectiveness are not the result of their being incompetent or bad. It is much easier, psychologically, for members to blame the invisible force called *culture*—as long as they take responsibility for changing it.

Here are some of the *new* norms that are often listed as necessary to help an organization adapt to modern times: Be willing to take on responsibility; initiate changes to improve performance; treat everyone with respect and as a source of valuable insight and expertise; congratulate those who suggest new ideas and new ways of doing things; enjoy your work and show your enthusiasm for a job well done; speak with pride about your work group; be helpful and supportive of the other groups in the organization; don't criticize the organization in front of clients or customers.

### Step Three: Identifying Culture-Gaps

The difference between the desired norms listed in Step Two and the actual norms listed in Step One can be dramatic. This difference is termed a *culture-gap*. The Kilmann-Saxton Culture-Gap Survey (1983) is a measurement tool that can be used to detect the gap between what the current culture is and what it should be.

The survey was developed by collecting more than 400 norms from employees in more than twenty-five different types of organizations. These norms were then organized as paired opposites in order to draw attention to contrasting normative pressures in the work situation. Here is an example of a norm pair: (*A*) share information only when it benefits your own work group versus (*B*) share information to help other groups. Each employee is asked to select the item in (*A*) or (*B*) that indicates, first, the pressures the work group puts on its members (actual norms) and, second, the norms that should be operating to promote high performance and morale (desired norms). The final set of twenty-eight norm pairs that appear on the survey was derived from statistical analysis of norms that were most frequently cited.

The first organizations that participated in research studies to develop the Kilmann-Saxton Culture-Gap Survey were all from the United States. The instrument was later used in various European nations, too, with the survey translated into the appropriate language, such as Dutch, Finnish, French, German, and Spanish. While the survey was used cross-culturally with great caution (since national cultures can be expected to affect corporate cultures), all experience to date has demonstrated the international relevance of four types of culture-gaps, each revealed through seven norm pairs:

- Task Support—norms having to do with information sharing, helping other groups, and concern with efficiency. Example: "Support the work of other groups" versus "Put down the work of other groups."
- Task Innovation—norms for being creative, applying different approaches, and doing new things. Example: "Always try to improve" versus "Don't rock the boat."
- Social Relationships—norms for socializing with one's work group and mixing friendships with business. Example: "Get to know the people in your work group" versus "Don't bother."
- Personal Freedom—norms for self-expression, exercising discretion, and pleasing oneself. Example: "Live for yourself and your family" versus "Live for your job and career."

As shown in Figure 5, these four culture-gaps are defined by two independent distinctions: technical versus human and short term versus long term. The technical/human distinction contrasts norms that guide the technical aspects of work in organizations with norms that guide the social and personal aspects. The short-term/long-term distinction contrasts norms that focus on day-to-day concerns versus norms that directly affect the future of the organization. The latter set includes norms that emphasize work improvements (rather than just getting today's work done) and norms that define the relationship between the individual and the organization (rather than focusing on daily social interactions). Since these two basic distinctions cover such a broad spectrum of experience in an organization, the resulting four types of culture-gaps are expected to capture the great variety of cultural norms that affect organizational success.

A work group, a department, a division, or an entire organization can be surveyed with regard to its culture-gaps. By calculating the differences between the actual norms and the desired

**Figure 5. The Four Culture-Gaps®.**

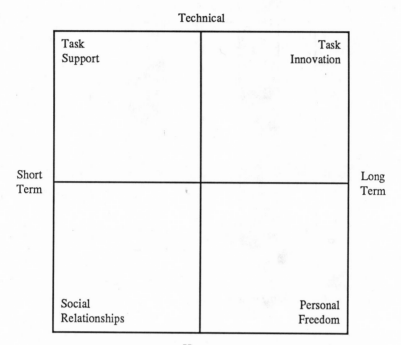

Technical

| | |
|---|---|
| Task<br>Support | Task<br>Innovation |
| Social<br>Relationships | Personal<br>Freedom |

Short Term ... Long Term

Human

*Source:* Reprinted from *The Kilmann-Saxton Culture-Gap Survey* by permission of Organizational Design Consultants. Copyright © 1983.

norms, four culture-gap scores are obtained. The larger the gap, the greater the likelihood that the current norms are hindering both morale and performance. If the assessed culture-gaps are allowed to continue, work groups are likely to resist any attempt at work improvements and offer lip service when changes in strategic direction are announced. Even corporate efforts to improve members' satisfaction and morale will be met with either apathy or active resistance.

Figure 6 shows how culture-gaps are displayed as a profile for easy interpretation. Each work group calculates its four average scores and then transfers them onto the appropriate bar graph, creating the profile. A positive culture-gap score is plotted as a filled

### Figure 6. Culture-Gap® Profile.

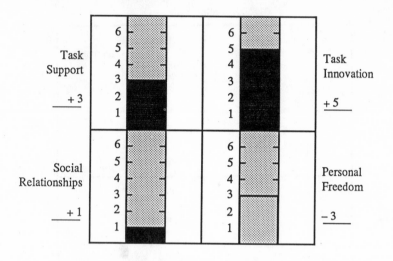

bar (+.1 to +7), a negative culture-gap score is plotted as an unfilled bar (-.1 to -7), and a zero score is simply ignored. A positive culture-gap score means that organizational success would be improved by changing the actual norms toward *more* Task Support, Task Innovation, or whatever is being considered. A negative culture-gap score means that *less* of that quality is desired for organizational success.

As revealed by the culture-gap profile shown in Figure 6, the technical norms of this work group do not encourage the necessary information sharing and support for getting the day-to-day work done. Even more pronounced, the actual norms do not encourage the innovative behavior that is required. Yet the work group believes that the current norms fostering social interaction are essentially the same as what is desired. Regarding Personal Freedom, perhaps there is too much discretion in following rules and regulations, and members realize that a closer adherence to organizational guidelines is necessary for success. Since three of the four culture-gaps reach a significant level (defined as three or more difference points), a broad-based problem is evident: The work group's culture is holding back morale and performance in several ways.

Using the Kilmann-Saxton Culture-Gap Survey in numerous profit and nonprofit organizations has revealed distinctive patterns of culture-gaps. In certain high-tech firms, for example, lack of cooperation and information sharing among groups has resulted in serious culture-gaps in Task Support. In the automotive and steel industries, not fostering creativity has resulted in big culture-gaps in Task Innovation. In some social service agencies, where workloads can vary greatly, large *negative* gaps in Social Relationships are found, indicating that too much time is spent socializing rather than getting the next job done. In extremely bureaucratic organizations, such as community and government agencies, large gaps in Personal Freedom are often evident, suggesting that members feel restricted by red tape and paperwork.

The most salient finding is the widespread presence of large culture-gaps in Task Innovation. It seems that companies all over the world are beset by significant differences between actual and desired norms in this area. An industrial culture that pushes for short-term financial results is bound to foster norms against efforts at long-term work improvements—regardless of what the formal documents and publicity statements claim. In the 1950s and 1960s, when many organizations operated in regulated, domestic, noncompetitive environments, members could perform their tasks in the same way year after year and still achieve organizational success. In today's world, however, innovation and constant improvement are mandatory for survival, let alone success.

Do all members in the same organization see the same culture-gaps? Apparently not. The smallest culture-gaps are found at the top of the organization's hierarchy. Executives believe their own publicity. They say, for example, that they foster creativity and innovation—as "shown" by the widely distributed brochures on the company's new innovation program—but do not recognize that their actions speak louder than their words. Culture-gaps are largest at the bottom levels of the organization, where employees experience the inconsistencies that have trickled down the hierarchy. Using the example of the innovation program, employees probably view it as a joke: "Innovation? You've got to be kidding. Nobody here even remembers the last time someone was rewarded for a new idea. If someone *did* propose something new, she wouldn't be here long to talk about it!"

Just as the *size* of culture-gaps can vary according to the shape of the organization pyramid, the *type* of culture-gaps can differ division by division in the same organization. Divisions have different histories, critical incidents, strategies, markets, and managers. Wallach (1983, p. 33) vividly depicts how different cultural norms can thrive in the same organization:

> Organizational cultures are not monolithic. Although strong cultures will be pervasive throughout an organization, coloring each employee's reality of the company's "personality," many cultures exist within the corporate reality. We all work for the same company, but the norms will vary somewhat from division to division, location to location, and functional area to functional area. Just as we are all Americans and share similar values, regional differences exist. Consider the stereotypical differences between a cowboy from Houston and a Brooks Brothers Bostonian. They look different, act different, and their values are different. Relocate a New Englander to Southern California and what do you have? Culture shock! What might be totally appropriate behavior in one functional/divisional/geographical piece of your company might be totally inappropriate in another.

The Kilmann-Saxton Culture-Gap Survey reveals that the divisions of the same organization have different cultures and, in fact, displays the pattern of culture-gaps throughout the organization. Figure 7 shows an organizational culture-gap profile—a summary picture of the four culture-gaps for each work unit in the form of an organization chart. This profile is a convenient way to see if the organization has the same culture-gaps in every unit or if units have some very different profiles. One should not assume that a firm currently has (or should have) only one culture. It all depends

Figure 7. Organizational Culture-Gap® Profile.

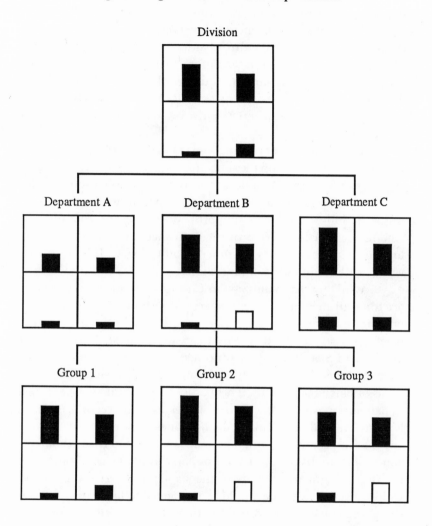

*Source:* Reprinted from *The Kilmann-Saxton Culture-Gap Survey* by permission of Organizational Design Consultants. Copyright © 1983.

on the nature of the work to be done and on just what behavior is required for success in each work unit.

A special problem emerges, however, when each division of a company has different cultural norms. Communications and conflicts among divisions are more difficult to manage. The divisions have different jargon, values, work habits, and attitudes. If divisions need to share information, technology, personnel, and other resources, the different cultures will get in the way of cooperation.

There is a general rule that can resolve this cultural dilemma: Let each division develop the subculture that is conducive to its own high performance and morale, but encourage each division to adopt those organization-wide norms that promote organizational success. The following norms support cooperation and coordination among the divisions: Help other departments whenever possible; look at the problem from the other's point of view; remember that we all work for the same organization.

While the Kilmann-Saxton Culture-Gap Survey is useful in teaching all members the language and meaning of norms, every organization has unique cultural qualities that cannot be anticipated in a standardized questionnaire. During Step One (actual norms) and Step Two (desired norms) of the culture track, group members often list norms that are unique to their organization in terms of language or focus. These unique norms can also be shown as paired opposites: Show favoritism versus treat everyone equally; be secretive and deceitful versus be honest and open; don't trust anyone who is not in your clique versus feel free to trust whomever you wish. Any list of unique norm pairs would be combined with the twenty-eight norm pairs of the standardized Kilmann-Saxton Culture-Gap Survey and would be responded to by the members in the same manner. Only by making these unique norms explicit can the members develop a deep understanding of their culture-gaps.

### Step Four: Closing Culture-Gaps

When members and their culture are at least open to change, it is miraculous how survey results or lists of desired norms affect the members of a work unit. As noted earlier, there is often a great sense of relief as people realize that they can live according to different norms and have the power to change their work environment. Surprisingly, some change can be brought about just by listing new norms because members start acting them out immediately after they are discussed.

When the members and their culture are cynical and depressed—as when the social energy in the organization has been deactivated—the response to survey results or lists of desired norms is quite different. Even when large culture-gaps are shown to exist, the members are often listless. They say that *their* work unit cannot change until the level of management above them changes. They believe that their external work environment is keeping them down.

When a culture-gap survey is conducted at the next-highest level, the very same arguments are heard again: "We have no power to change; we have to wait for the next level to let us change; *they* have the power." It is astonishing, after conducting a culture-gap survey for the entire organization, to present the results to top management only to find the same feelings of helplessness. In this case top management is waiting for the economy to change! In reality, it is the corporate culture that is saying: Don't take on responsibility; protect yourself at all costs; don't try to change until everyone else has changed; don't lead the way, follow; if you ignore the problem, maybe it'll go away.

This is a perfect example of a company in a culture rut—the shock of acknowledging the discrepancy between actual and desired norms is just too great to confront. Instead, the organization buries its head in the sand and hopes everything will sort itself out. Even in the face of strong evidence of a serious problem, this organizational denial persists. And it is a much more powerful and perhaps more destructive force than any individual denial. The *group's* power to define reality clouds each person's better judgment.

Recall the distinction between external and internal control (Rotter, 1971) presented in Chapter Two. A culture rut is rooted in external control: Everyone expects others to control what happens, which eventually makes everyone feel powerless and inept. An adaptive culture, however, is based on internal control: If managers and members decide that change *should* occur, then changes can be brought about. Control is a social reality, not an objective reality.

Many organizations have achieved great success even though everyone else "knew" this was impossible.

Merely listing and stating the desired norms, however, is not sufficient to instill them in the organization. Each work group must develop a *sanctioning system* that monitors and enforces the desired norms. Essentially, if there are no penalties for persisting in old ways and no reward for engaging in new behavior, why would anyone want to change? Thus before the reward system—the fifth track—provides formal incentives to individuals for behaving according to new norms, each work group develops an *informal* reward system.

Specifically, each work group is asked to decide what exactly will be done if a group member acts out an old norm (a "violation") or engages in a desired behavior (a "victory"). Suppose, for example, the actual norm is "Arrive at meetings whenever you feel like it" and the desired norm is "Arrive at meetings on time." The first infraction usually results in subtle reminders—group members may conspicuously look at their watches when a member arrives late to a meeting. Subsequent infractions incur stronger sanctions— placing someone's punctuality problem on the formal meeting agenda, for example, or noting the incident on the employees' bulletin board. Punctual members may even be treated to a lavish dinner by those who have violated the norm!

So long as the sanctioning system developed by each work group is ethical and legal, every group can be encouraged to use their imagination in rewarding desired behavior and penalizing outmoded habits. If each sanctioning system also involves gentle humor, the cultural change will not be as difficult as might be expected. What if group members insist they are too mature for such a "social game"? Undoubtedly they have failed to grasp the extent to which their work groups have been using powerful sanctions to maintain the status quo. Unconscious sanctions such as "one mistake and you're out" are more debilitating than the sanctioning systems that are devised during the culture track: Bringing the long-standing sanctioning systems to the attention of group members generally motivates them to create an open system that is more equitable.

In one major company implementing the culture track, for

example, a management group suggested that each new norm should be written on an index card and given a number. Each member in the group was then responsible for monitoring several norms and calling attention to outmoded behavior. Eventually, group members no longer needed to cite the norms—only the numbers. Members would state: "You just committed a number twelve" or "You pulled a seven on me." These people were able to enforce their new norms in a lighthearted manner, yet the point of adopting the norms was made unequivocally. When outsiders heard such interchanges they were confused—and this added to the group's cohesiveness, since the members now had their own secret code.

In another major company, top executives designed their sanctioning system by humorously making use of the corporate pins of the American eagle that they proudly wore on their lapels. The first time a group member violated a norm, one wing of the eagle would be broken off *and* the executive still would have to wear the pin as before. The second time an infraction occurred, the other wing of the eagle would be broken off. Thus, after two infractions, the slow-to-change executive would be wearing the pin of the eagle, showing the body of the bird but not the wings. And if that was not enough to persuade the executive to change his ways, the third time this person violated the norm he would have to sit in the corner of the room, facing the wall, during the next staff meeting! Although this third sanction probably was never applied, every executive got the point: Behavior *had* to change, particularly to set a proper example for the rest of the membership.

### Step Five: Sustaining Cultural Change

The first four steps of the culture track can be conducted in just one or two workshop sessions. If there is to be significant behavioral change throughout the organization, however, continual reinforcement, subsequent reminders, and more group discussions are needed to sustain what has begun in these early sessions.

There are three overlapping phases of behavioral change that clarify what takes place during the culture track: unfreezing, change, and refreezing (Lewin, 1951). The *unfreezing phase* occurs when group members recognize that their behavior needs to change, as revealed by their self-assessed culture-gaps. The members also accept that their new sanctioning system must be applied if there is to be any real incentive for change. But knowing something intellectually is not the same as behaving differently.

The *change phase* occurs when members begin to behave according to the new cultural norms: Now members share information with other groups, arrive at all group meetings on time, and offer opposing viewpoints during group discussions. Behaving in these new ways is initially awkward and forced. Anybody who attempts to break an old habit and replace it with something new will feel strange at first. The easiest thing to do is revert back to the old habit even if it violates new norms and results in various sanctions. It is also much easier to wait for the other person to change rather than take, on one's own, those first embarrassing steps.

The *refreezing phase* occurs when the new ways of behaving on the job become more natural and automatic. Members no longer need to remind one another of the desired norms: The new behavior has developed into new habits. It now takes less effort (and less anxiety) to enact the new norms.

Progressing from unfreezing through change to refreezing, however, takes a lot of time. From the start of the culture track, perhaps four to six months will pass before members have significantly modified their behavior. Members quickly discover that it is a big jump from talk to action—from workshop discussions to behavioral changes on the job. Often there is a great deal of frustration when members expect a cultural change to take place immediately. Even when they admit that they themselves have not done anything differently, they still wait for something to happen quickly. Putting these experiences in terms of "unfreezing, change, and refreezing" helps alleviate the pressure for instant success. But putting these same experiences in terms of "external and internal control" also encourages everyone to proceed with definite action— while being patient with others.

In order to move the change process along, follow-up workshop sessions are conducted for each work group in the improvement program, at least every other month. Moreover, the work groups are asked to have several meetings at the workplace, in between these formal workshops, in order to continue their cultural discussions. In these subsequent workshop sessions and on-the-job discussions, work groups are asked to address several questions: What has improved? What has stayed the same? What has become worse? Attention then focuses on pinpointing the obstacles that are blocking cultural change—or, more precisely, understanding the *causes* of what is preventing members from translating awareness into action. Next, numerous solutions are derived that can remove these obstacles to cultural change. When the best solutions have been chosen, action steps are developed to implement the solutions—as soon as possible. During the next group meeting, the members again inquire about the success of their efforts (by indicating what has improved, stayed the same, or become worse), and the cycle continues.

This cycle of cultural problem solving works best if each work group puts together a detailed written report analyzing their culture-gaps and documenting their sanctioning system. The very act of writing this report forces members to express their understanding of the causes and consequences of culture-gaps, to organize their action plans, and to commit their intentions on paper. And with the written report in every group member's possession, it is not necessary to reestablish prior agreements on norms and sanctioning systems every time the group meets for further discussion. Instead, the group can concentrate on how well its intentions have been realized. Note, however, that often there is considerable resistance to writing these reports and distributing them to members of the group. Perhaps the report writing reminds some people of the tedious homework they had to do for school—when they did not fully appreciate that learning new approaches demands disciplined analysis and practice. Group members can be encouraged to participate in this educational process, however, and can be given various reading materials to enhance their understanding of cultural change.

As the process advances well into the change phase, it becomes more and more difficult for anyone to act out the old norms without receiving a public reprimand. In my experience, the greatest pressure to change is on the middle levels of the organization. First the pressure comes from top managers who are determined to set the right example for their subordinates. With top management's commitment, the pressure on middle management will be very considerable indeed.

The pressure on middle management also comes from the rank and file. These members are quick to adopt new ways of doing things and often are the first members to change—they have been waiting a long time for more freedom and involvement in their work. Usually, the lower-level employees discover that the culture track is a refreshing change from the routine of their daily job assignments. As a result, they are eager to become involved in this new activity (as long as they believe it is for real) and, in fact, delight in moving forward more quickly than their managers.

As the process of change moves into the refreezing phase, the new norms become internalized—sustaining the change. Approximately six to nine months after the culture track was initiated, the Kilmann-Saxton Culture-Gap Survey can be administered again to assess which cultural segments of the organization have improved, stayed the same, or become worse. Each work group then analyzes its own culture-gap results to consider what additional work needs to be done in order to bring all culture-gaps within tolerable limits.

Figure 8 shows culture-gap comparisons for a division of a large industrial corporation before the culture track was initiated and six months later. As the profile illustrates, the culture-gap for Task Support, the most troublesome for the division of 217 members, was virtually cut in half (from 4.5 down to 2.3 on a 7.0 scale). The gap for Task Innovation also decreased for the division as a whole, but not so dramatically (from 3.5 down to 2.4). Both the gaps for Social Relationships and Personal Freedom remained as insignificant as before. This division-wide pattern of culture-gap comparisons was similar throughout most departments and work groups in the division, suggesting that a more adaptive culture was developing. Only a few work groups still had problems in Task Support and Task Innovation that required further attention.

### The Bottom Line

An adaptive culture sets the stage for all other improvement efforts, including the remaining four tracks of the program. In

**Figure 8. Culture-Gap® Comparisons.**

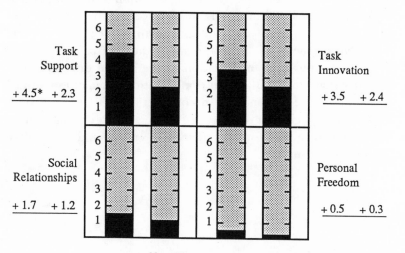

$N$ = 177 respondents

*Number on left is from first administration of survey (December 1982); number on right is from second administration (June 1983).

*Source:* Adapted from *The Kilmann-Saxton Culture-Gap Survey* by permission of Organizational Design Consultants. Copyright © 1983.

contrast, a dysfunctional culture, breeding a lack of trust, confidence, and the sharing of information, makes it nearly impossible to improve anything.

Only in an adaptive culture will managers be willing to accept their shortcomings and learn new ways to address complex problems; they need an adaptive culture to recognize the many changes going on in the setting and to uncover and update everyone's assumptions. In an adaptive culture, the membership can participate in team-building efforts to improve the quality of decisions and actions on complex problems, where a collaborative effort is essential. Only in an adaptive culture will the membership be able to examine and then modify the formally documented systems—strategy-structure and reward system—representing very sensitive and crucial problems.

Note, however, that the new culture will gradually revert to its old dysfunctional ways if it is not supported by the remaining four tracks. The management skills and team-building tracks will instill the right leadership style in each work unit to support an adaptive culture. With the strategy-structure track, the formally documented systems will be working with the informal work-group pressures to move the organization in the desired direction. The reward system track will design compensation schemes to monitor and support the new norms in conjunction with the informal sanctioning systems. In these ways, the social energy, management style, team spirit, and formal systems will create—and maintain—organizational success.

# 4

# The Management Skills Track:

## Learning How to
## Manage Complex Problems

Many of today's managers, though they may deny or not realize it, are members of a flourishing movement I call "the Panacean Conspiracy." These managers, typically promoted into management from such technical specialties as engineering, law, or finance, have little managerial know-how. Most don't have the time, interest, or awareness needed to learn their new craft, but they are anxious to produce immediately. What they are looking for, although they may profess to know better, are quick-fix solutions to dynamic, complex problems.
—Mayer, 1983, p. 23

What mix of management skills is required for successful performance? It all depends on one's position in the organization. The importance of technical skills predominates at the bottom of the management hierarchy, supported by social, interpersonal, and motor skills (manual dexterity). At the top of the organization pyramid, leadership, administrative, and analytical skills are most important for successful performance, supported by people management skills. Therefore, as members move up in the hierarchy, they will need to develop different skills.

Many times I have observed the workings of the Peter Principle—the theory that managers rise to the highest level of their incompetence (Peter and Hull, 1969). Because of excellent performance at one level, employees are promoted to the next level. This process continues until poor performance results from the gap between the employee's current skills and the skills actually needed for the new job. The classic example is promoting an engineer to a management position because of her excellent technical skills and performance—only to find that she continues her efforts in the technical domain and ignores the management domain. Correcting this situation first requires an understanding of what the new management job entails. Then the right kind of classroom and on-the-job training must be provided so that the former engineer will develop management skills.

The theme of the management skills track is this: A different set of skills is required for managing a complex hologram than for managing a simple machine. Leadership, analytical, and interpersonal skills must be developed explicitly to handle dynamic complexity. In a nutshell, if managers are selected and trained to handle largely simple, well-structured, predefined problems—viewing the world as a simple machine—the entire organization will reach its highest level of incompetence.

This chapter presents the means for learning to manage complex problems—which include organizational problems (addressed throughout the team-building, strategy-structure, and reward system tracks) as well as the firm's technical and business problems. First, we will consider the five steps of problem management. These steps demonstrate that today's managers must be more than just decision makers or problem solvers: Dynamic complexity requires that managers first sense and define problems before they can select and implement solutions. Second, we will examine four personality types. These types characterize the different ways that managers assimilate information and make decisions: A manager's personality type determines what step in problem management will be overemphasized and what steps will be undervalued. Knowing how personality influences problem management will encourage each member to compensate both for his natural inclinations and for his acknowledged limitations. Third, we will see how the method of assumptional analysis is used for managing the most complex aspects of problem management:

defining problems and implementing solutions. Everyone in the management skills track is taught the skills for surfacing and debating the critical assumptions that underlie different problem definitions and implementation plans. It is through this process of assumptional analysis that a holographic world comes to life for those who are prepared to manage it.

## Learning Problem Management

Once the various activities in the culture track have enabled all the managers to accept the need for change and improvement, they will be eager to learn new management skills. If their skills for managing people are deficient (skills in communicating, providing feedback, resolving conflicts, and managing groups), some basic training is needed before they are ready to learn skills for managing problems. The full diagnosis of the organization's problems and opportunities as discussed in Chapter Two provides the criteria for designing all activities in the management skills track.

The best place to learn the skills for problem management and assumptional analysis is in a workshop setting. There the managers (sometimes including key professionals and potential managers) are removed from the daily pressures of their jobs and from the authority of their immediate superiors. Generally it takes several workshop sessions, conducted by skilled internal or external consultants (instructors) over a period of several months, for all managers to acquire new skills. During this period, managers learn new skills by practicing with cases and exercises before tackling real problems. But just as the culture track encourages all members to behave in the workplace according to the desired norms, every manager is encouraged to apply his new management skills to all his business and technical problems—even before the team-building track begins.

Figure 9 shows the five steps of problem management: sensing problems, defining problems, deriving solutions, implementing solutions, and evaluating outcomes. After these steps are conducted, the cycle repeats if something still needs attention.

Figure 9. The Five Steps of Problem Management.

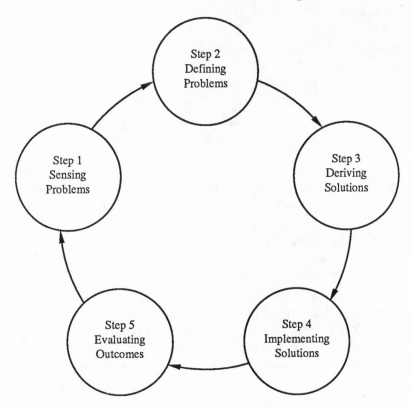

*Step One: Sensing Problems*

The workshop participants are taught that the cycle of problem management begins when someone in the organization senses that something is wrong. A problem is defined as a gap between what is (actual performance) and what should be (desired performance). If this gap is big enough, a problem is sensed. For example, the expected turnover rate in a company may be 15 percent a year. But if the turnover rate reaches 25 percent, somebody may well realize that something needs to be done, since this rate significantly exceeds the acceptable range.

Any number of indicators, both formal and informal, can be

used to sense whether a problem exists: increased cost of providing services, smaller appropriation of resources, decrease in clientele, smaller market share, more companies providing the same products or services, lower earnings per share, high turnover or absenteeism, or increase in consumer complaints. Aside from these "hard" measures, any sign of a culture rut (discussed in the previous chapter) may signal a significant problem—general apathy, resistance, anxiety, frustration, disruptive behavior. Once an indicator crosses the threshold of what is considered acceptable, members in the organization usually sense that a problem exists.

Denying the existence of a problem is a *sensing error*: the likelihood that a problem exists but is not recognized. The other side of the sensing error is when the organization believes that there is a problem when in fact there is not. Here the organization may be too sensitive to minor fluctuations in various indicators and therefore tends to initiate problem management efforts prematurely and unnecessarily. In this case, the worst that can happen is that time and resources are wasted when everything is really under control. Perhaps the organization should simply raise its threshold levels. But ultimately it does seem better to err by being too sensitive to emerging problems than to ignore the really crucial ones.

At this early point in the learning process, participants in the workshop usually wonder just who is responsible for sensing all their company's problems: Does their organization sense problems in a purposeful and systematic way? When they realize, as they often do, that problem sensing has been conducted ad hoc, the managers begin to suggest specific systems for ensuring that important problems are not being overlooked or denied, simply because everyone believes that someone else, somehow, must be addressing them.

### Step Two: Defining Problems

Once it is sensed that a problem exists, the next step is to discover just what the problem is. Is the organization's high turnover rate the result of interpersonal conflicts, a culture rut, low job commitment, few promotion opportunities, competitive job offers from other firms, unfulfilled salary promises, a lack of clarity

in job descriptions, or boring work? Any of these problem definitions (or several of them) could be the reason behind the high
turnover rate. Essentially, the problem definition is viewed as the
*cause*, in contrast to the *symptom*, for an indicator crossing a
threshold. Symptoms are the results that occur in any stakeholder
(switches in buying behavior, decreases in market share, declining
morale), while the definition of the problem is the reason these
results took place (a change in a competitor's strategy, the
introduction of a new product, a change in the compensation
system). The objective of this step, therefore, is to work backward
from the symptom to determine what caused it.

A *defining error* can be described as the likelihood of
addressing the wrong problem or working on a trivial problem
rather than the most important problem—given the organization's
mission and its setting. How do managers usually define problems?
More often than not, they assume that their view of the world (their
specialty) defines the essence of the problem. This selective
perception is natural for anyone who has received extensive training
in one skill area. Professionals wear blinders in order to become
specialists: A finance person sees a financial world; a marketing
person sees a marketing world; a social scientist sees a world of
human interaction. This biasing effect is reinforced by one's
personality (the traits and abilities that incline one to pursue a
specialty in the first place) and by one's work group (which puts
pressure on members to see problems a certain way).

*Any* problem definition arrived at through tunnel vision can
result in a defining error. Strangely, a particular definition of the
problem is often assumed because that is the way it has always been
addressed—even if the problem never is resolved. This habitual
tendency is illustrated by the executive who always defines a
problem of low performance as a need for tighter controls over her
middle managers. Every time something goes wrong, she "tightens
the screws," but to no avail. Perhaps the middle managers need
*more* freedom to perform, not less, or perhaps low performance
results from any of a dozen other causes, but other problem
definitions are just not considered.

At this point in the learning process, workshop participants
begin to wonder just how much of their time on the job is spent

working on the wrong problem. Gradually they begin to see the pattern: Problems do not get solved to anyone's satisfaction; instead, the same endless discussions are heard again and again, year after year, without resolution. Everyone knows what everyone else will argue for or against on any given topic, but nobody bothers to understand *why* each expert has a different viewpoint, let alone *how* these different viewpoints can be synthesized into a correct problem definition.

### Step Three: Deriving Solutions

The next step for the managers to learn involves generating different solutions to the defined problem and then selecting the best of them. Managers must use their imagination and experience to construct alternative solutions. This is especially the case if the organization has continued to pick the same solutions again and again without a successful outcome. Some organizations, for example, always try to solve the "performance problem" by instituting a newly improved, special recognition program, even though it never works.

How can one choose among the proposed solutions? Making use of decision theory, probability assessment, and statistical analysis, one constructs a *decision tree*, with the problem as the stump of the tree and the alternatives as branches. Alongside each alternative branch are associated costs, benefits, and probabilities leading to the desired outcome. Sometimes several action steps follow beyond each first-level alternative, which results in branches leading off from other branches. Then a cost-benefit analysis is calculated for each series of branches so that the decision maker can choose a single—or integrated—solution. Thus the process of deriving solutions is more structured than the process of defining problems.

A *solving error*—the likelihood of selecting one alternative when another is in fact better—can be made when it comes to choosing among two or more solutions to a problem. I am assuming, of course, that a defining error has not been committed and the full range of possible alternative solutions has been generated. If, for example, a defining error *has* been committed, then worrying about a solving error is misplaced precision. It is far better to select a weak solution to the right problem than to choose the best solution to the wrong problem.

The following story often helps managers see the fundamental differences between defining problems and deriving solutions and between defining errors and solving errors. The story takes place in the marketing department of a large industrial corporation, where virtually all the middle managers were complaining that they did not have the necessary information to make good decisions about introducing new products in the marketplace. Sensing an important problem, a senior executive contacted the company's information-systems department. Not surprisingly, this technically oriented unit offered three alternative computer systems to solve the problem. While the alternative systems differed according to size and flexibility, each was shockingly expensive and required considerable training for the user.

As the executive was deciding on these alternative systems, he happened to mention his problem to a psychologist who worked for the corporate planning staff. The psychologist suggested that the problem might be more human than technical—maybe the managers were complaining about their lack of information as a way of discounting their responsibility for making risky decisions involving huge sums of money. Defining the problem in these terms, she offered two alternative solutions: Modify the reward system to emphasize long-term results rather than single mistakes in new product introductions or require groups of managers to sign off on these decisions rather than separate individuals.

Although the executive was intrigued by these suggestions, he decided to go ahead with one of the computer systems, since it promised more, better, and quicker information. After all, this is what his managers had complained about. But even though it took only a few months to install the system, the managers showed little enthusiasm. While somewhat disappointed with this response, the executive assumed that their attitude would change as soon as the system was in use.

It was never to be. Even one year after the system was in operation, very few managers were using it. In fact, fewer than half of them had bothered to attend any of the training sessions. From what the executive could see, his managers continued to make their decisions just as before—but now they complained that R&D was not providing quality products for them to promote, which made their work even more difficult.

Fed up with the endless complaining, the executive was now willing to try one of the suggestions the psychologist had offered almost two years ago. He decided to institute a new procedure for signing off on large promotional expenses by using group decision making (five to ten managers). The results were astonishing. Within a short time, the managers became much more enthusiastic about the prospects for the new products coming out of R&D. As a group, they also developed more creative ways to promote these products—such as establishing a consumer panel in their own community.

With this change in attitude, the executive began pushing his managers to use the expensive computer system that had been installed. The managers responded: "Why would we want to use a system that cranks out endless reams of statistical calculations? We can collect the information much faster by questioning our consumer panel!"

This story illustrates how various problem definitions not only address the same situation differently but result in vastly different solutions. Choosing the "technical" definition (needing more information) versus the "human" definition (avoiding responsibility) is an example of a *defining* error (in choosing a wrong decision tree). Once the problem is defined, selecting a weak solution with regard to cost-benefit considerations is an example of a *solving* error (in choosing a wrong branch on a decision tree—requiring major reward system changes rather than making simple changes in decision procedures). Overlooking or deliberately ignoring one or more decision trees drastically restricts the range of potential solutions. Furthermore, while simple problems consist of just one decision tree (the problem is fully understood by only one specialty), complex problems have multiple decision trees (each specialty has a different perspective on cause and effect in a complex situation).

Figure 10 shows a graphic representation of the numerous decision trees—including their respective branches—that can be

Figure 10. Complex Problems and Decision Trees.

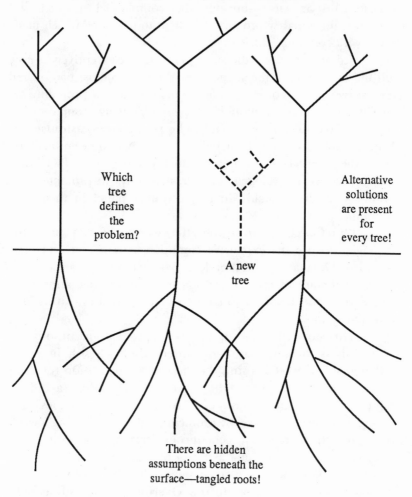

Which tree defines the problem?

Alternative solutions are present for every tree!

A new tree

There are hidden assumptions beneath the surface—tangled roots!

found in the forest of complex problems. While decision trees usually are drawn from left to right (as if they were lying on their sides), I find it more useful to draw them from the ground up—alive and growing. The primary benefit of drawing decision trees in this holographic manner, however, is to see that not only are they directly observable above the surface of experience, but each tree is rooted—grounded—in its below-the-surface assumptions. As the participants in the management skills track will learn shortly, before one can understand why different experts define complex problems according to different decision trees, it is necessary to expose their underlying assumptions. Then, by untangling the roots of several different decision trees, it is possible to create an altogether new—hybrid—decision tree in the forest (as shown by the dotted lines). Above all, this synthesized decision tree offers completely new alternative solutions—branches—that none of the original trees could ever have revealed.

At this point in the learning process, managers often mention a vicious cycle that persists in their organization: The pressure for short-term results pushes them to jump repeatedly from one branch to another on the *same* decision tree—without, of course, even considering alternative trees, let alone examining the roots (assumptions) underlying their favorite tree. Sometimes the corporate culture encourages this knee-jerk response to problems by the following unwritten rule: Don't just stand there, do something! Once the managers recognize the importance of defining problems before solutions are chosen, the desired cultural norm becomes: Don't just do something, stand there! Naturally, the phrase "stand there" is meant to convey that managers should take the time to discover and analyze *different* decision trees before they dive into action. This revelation is a radical experience for many managers. They recognize that defining errors *and* solving errors are likely to result from blind adherence to only one decision tree. The managers now agree to include different experts—decision trees—in their subsequent discussions of complex problems.

### Step Four: Implementing Solutions

It is one thing to derive what appears to be the best solution and quite another to implement it in the organization. There are many examples of excellent solutions that were implemented poorly, at the wrong time, or by the wrong people. Implementation should not be taken for granted: Never assume that a good solution will automatically be accepted and used.

Failing to anticipate obstacles, resistance, and forces operating to keep things the same results in an *implementing error*: the likelihood of not implementing a solution properly. No matter how well the other steps have been conducted and to what extent the other errors have been minimized, committing an implementing error will nullify the total effort at problem management.

Remember the story of the marketing department? Most workshop participants realize that an implementing error occurred when the executive decided to install a computer system but did not ask his middle managers about their preferences regarding its design. Moreover, the managers in the story may have had some anxieties about learning a computerized way of processing information. Certainly there was a critical assumption behind installing the computer system—that the managers would be motivated to use it. Workshop participants begin to recognize that ignoring the intricate technical features and the many psychological factors that affect the use of a solution typically results in an implementing error in their own organization.

### Step Five: Evaluating Outcomes

Did the implemented solution actually solve the problem? If the indicators are no longer beyond threshold levels, the organization may assume that the problem has been managed properly. But the initial problem may have stirred up new problems, and these might motivate the organization to continue the problem management cycle. Alternatively, if the initial problem is still sensed after the organization has gone through all five steps, it is likely that one or more steps were performed incorrectly and that one or more errors were committed. After a full study has been made, each step in which an error is detected should be performed again. Continuing through this cycle should resolve the initial problem and any emerging problems.

Now back to the story of the marketing department. Workshop participants notice that the constant complaining by the marketing managers disappeared soon after the last solution was implemented (instituting a group procedure for signing off on large promotional expenses). But a new problem emerged as a result of previous errors in problem management—implementing the wrong solution to the wrong problem (installing a computer system to provide more information about new product introductions). Workshop participants begin to wonder what could be done with the expensive equipment that lay idle. They suggest that the executive and his marketing managers could apply the five steps of problem management to determine the best use of the computer.

After the workshop participants have practiced each step of problem management with various cases and exercises, they insist that it is no longer acceptable to continue on their merry-go-round of impulsive action that never solves the real problems. The managers now develop their own definition of organizational success: solving each complex problem in one cycle of problem management—doing it right the first time.

## Four Personalities for Problem Management

While struggling with organizational problems, managers spend most of their time assimilating information and making decisions. But there are different ways of doing these things, depending on the manager's personality traits and the nature of the problem itself. While we have been concentrating on the different steps involved in managing complex problems, we now consider how different personality types determine whether due time and attention are given to each step of the process.

The personality typology of Jung (1923) has been shown to be exceedingly useful in explaining the effect of individual differences on organizational behavior. Specifically, Jung's framework contends that people have different ways of taking in information and then making decisions.

There are two basic ways in which people take in information: sensation and intuition. Sensation refers to the preference for taking in information directly by the five senses. It focuses on the details, facts, and specifics of a situation, the here and now, the hard data, the itemized parts—what can be seen, touched, smelled, and so on. In contrast, intuition is a preference for the whole rather than the parts, for the possibilities, hunches, or future implications of a situation, the extrapolations, interpolations, and unique interrelationships among pieces of information—what cannot be seen or touched directly. Thus with intuition the focus is beyond the parts;

with sensation the focus is on the parts themselves. According to Jung, people develop a preference for one of either mode of taking in information. Although they can apply either sensation or intuition when required, they may be unable to do each equally well. In fact, the information-taking mode that is not preferred is regarded as a person's weaker function or "blind side."

There are two basic ways in which people arrive at decisions: thinking and feeling. Thinking refers to a very impersonal, logical, analytical preference for making a decision. If such and such is true, then this and that follow, based on a logical analysis. Feeling, in contrast, is a very personal, subjective, unique way of making a decision. Does the person *like* the alternative? Does it fit with her values and the image she has of herself? While the development of such a conclusion is not logical per se, it is not illogical either. Feeling is alogical—simply based on a different style of reaching decisions. Just as they do with sensation and intuition, people develop a preference for either thinking or feeling. Although they can apply either when required, they may be unsure of themselves when they rely on their blind side for decision making.

The two personality characteristics associated with information taking and decision making, as shown in Figure 11, result in four personality types: intuition-feeling (NF), intuition-thinking (NT), sensation-thinking (ST), and sensation-feeling (SF). Each personality type is most suitable for a different step of problem management.

The NF (intuition–feeling) person enjoys ambiguous situations. Such people prefer looking into the future—all the possibilities—and use very personal criteria for deciding what is important to consider. Such people thrive on dynamic complexity; they function best when there is a minimum of structure or when problems have not even been defined yet. Thus NF persons are most confident when dealing with Step One of problem management: sensing problems. Because of their preferences, however, they become uneasy when faced with the structured aspects of the process—their blind side.

The NT (intuition–thinking) person enjoys looking at a complex situation from many different—global—perspectives. Such people are attracted to abstract discussions; they get bored with

## Figure 11. The Jungian Dimensions of Personality.

**Thinking (T)**

(1) logical
(2) analytical
(3) scientific
(4) dispassionate
(5) cold
(6) impersonal
(7) concerned with matters of truth
(8) unconcerned with people's feelings
(9) theoretical
(10) concerned with rationality

**Sensation (S)**

(1) careful
(2) concerned with parts
(3) lives in present
(4) specialist
(5) factual
(6) precise
(7) concrete
(8) realist
(9) likes to develop a single idea in depth rather than several ideas
(10) practical

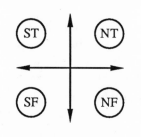

**Intuition (N)**

(1) risk taker
(2) concerned with whole
(3) lives in future
(4) generalist
(5) hypothetical
(6) vague
(7) speculative
(8) idealistic
(9) likes to produce many alternative ideas
(10) inventive

**Feeling (F)**

(1) alogical
(2) poetic
(3) artistic
(4) passionate
(5) warm
(6) personal
(7) concerned with matters of ethics
(8) concerned with people's feelings
(9) atheoretical
(10) concerned with justice

well-structured and routine problems, and they abhor details. NT persons, therefore, are most confident dealing with Step Two of problem management: defining problems. Investigating different problem definitions and then synthesizing them into one decision tree are facilitated by the NT's conceptual and theoretical ability. But because of their preference for thinking, NT persons require some analytical starting point—say, an indication that a problem already exists.

The ST (sensation-thinking) person enjoys the well-structured aspects of problem management. Such people choose a certain alternative on the basis of a logical, impersonal analysis. ST people seek single answers to most questions and prefer the answers to be clearly right or wrong according to some quantitative assessment (such as a cost-benefit calculation). It is not surprising, then, that ST persons are most confident dealing with Step Three of problem management: deriving solutions. They are less confident dealing with uncertainty, imprecision, subjective criteria, and personal interactions, but these qualities are not germane to deriving solutions.

The SF (sensation-feeling) person enjoys interpersonal interactions. This activity satisfies their preference for the immediate experience as well as for being with people. SF people are concerned with the special needs and aspirations of all their colleagues in the organization—rather than the technical or analytical aspects of problem management (ST or NT) or the broad aspects of problem sensing (NF). SF persons, therefore, are most confident when dealing with Step Four of problem management: implementing solutions. Their personal sensitivity and warmth enable them to feel how any solution might affect the quality of life for the organization's members.

These descriptions of personality types portray the *extremes.* One should not conclude that only NF persons can sense problems, only NTs can define problems, only STs can derive solutions, and only SFs can implement solutions. Rather, these preferences enable certain aspects of problem management to be performed better than others. It is not that STs cannot sense problems or implement solutions, but that an NF and SF, respectively, will be more natural at it and might do it a little better. But because NFs and STs are complete opposites of each other on both personality dimensions (information taking and decision making), STs will have trouble sensing problems while NFs will have their greatest challenge in calculating solutions. For the same reason, SFs will find it most taxing defining problems while NTs will struggle most with implementing solutions.

Participants in the management skills workshops can assess their own personality types by responding to the Myers-Briggs Type Indicator (Myers, 1962). In this way, each participant becomes aware of both his personality preferences and his blind spots. This knowledge helps each person compensate for his own strengths and limitations, not only during the workshops but on the job as well. Most managers recognize that interpersonal conflicts can sometimes be explained by the collision of opposite personality types. And a manager's reaction to problems can sometimes be explained by the fit—or lack of fit—between his preferences for assimilating information and making decisions and what steps of problem management he is asked to perform. Participants also note that the four personality types correspond to the four culture-gaps introduced in the culture track: STs are most affected by culture-gaps in Task Support; NTs are most bothered by gaps in Task Innovation; SFs are deeply affected by gaps in Social Relationships; NFs are most concerned with culture-gaps in Personal Freedom.

## Learning Assumptional Analysis

Assumptional analysis is a systematic method for addressing the most complex steps in problem management: defining problems and implementing solutions. The method not only reveals all the different decision trees that are relevant to problem definitions and implementation plans; it also probes below the surface of each tree to examine its roots—the hidden assumptions that keep each tree alive and well. It is through the use of different personality types and all the relevant areas of expertise that a synthesis of different decision trees and their roots can be obtained—thereby enabling managers to minimize defining errors and implementing errors. The other steps of problem management are often less complex since they require either "go" or "no go" decisions (sensing problems and evaluating outcomes) or well-structured, analytical approaches (deriving solutions).

The process for *learning* assumptional analysis consists of surfacing assumptions, classifying assumptions, and synthesizing assumptions. The culture track, remember, encourages the transfer of learning from the workshop to the workplace. The process of acquiring skills for assumptional analysis reinforces this same objective by using an ongoing-group exercise, which is described below, to deal directly with the transfer-of-learning problem.

### Surfacing Assumptions

Whenever someone concludes that her definition of the problem (or plan for implementation) is correct, her arguments are sound only if their underlying assumptions are true. Here we define *assumptions* as all the things one has to take for granted as true—human nature, mother nature, father time, and lady luck—in order to argue convincingly that the conclusion, as stated, is correct. We define *conclusion* as anything argued for or against, such as a plan, policy, problem definition, or implementation method.

Assumptional analysis requires a minimum of two very different conclusions in order to initiate the process. I have found it most advantageous to sort the managers into their four Jungian personality groups: All the STs are assigned to one group, all the NTs are assigned to another group, and so on. Composing the workshop groups according to personality types virtually guarantees the development of radically different conclusions, decision trees, and, hence, assumptions—exactly what is desired. For convenience, I will refer to such "conclusion groups" as *C-groups*.

Each C-group, usually consisting of three to ten persons, is assigned a separate room to examine one of the initial conclusions that have been proposed by others or developed by the groups themselves. These conclusions are *initial* because they will surely undergo change as their underlying assumptions are analyzed. Initial conclusions are just a way to start the process—a way of getting at the tried-and-true assumptions. In conducting the management skills track, each of the following four conclusions is assigned to a different C-group based on personality type: (1) We can apply to our jobs what we learn in these workshops. (2) We *cannot* apply to our jobs what we learn in these workshops. (3) This organization can be successful without any change at all. (4) This organization can be successful if each manager vows to do his very best. None of these extreme conclusions is apt to represent the whole truth. But by probing below the surface to untangle the assumptional roots beneath all decision trees, one can arrive at a deeper understanding of the transfer-of-learning problem.

The assumptions underlying a conclusion can be surfaced by listing all the potential stakeholders, both inside and outside the organization, who are involved in the conclusion and who therefore have a stake in what happens. The primary reason for identifying stakeholders is not to list people and groups for its own sake, but to surface assumptions. The objective is not to miss *any* relevant individual, group, or organization. Managers implicitly make assumptions about what the various stakeholders want, believe, expect, and value—how stakeholders make decisions or engage in actions themselves.

The four personality-based C-groups usually list the following stakeholders: each person himself, superiors, subordinates, peers in one's own group, peers in other groups, top management, unions, stockholders, future managers, future employees, competitors, customers, and the workshop instructor. Since each C-group's list of stakeholders is always amazingly similar to the other C-groups', managers immediately develop confidence in their ability to continue learning assumptional analysis. Furthermore, they begin to realize that, in the past, they included only a few stakeholders in their implicit analysis of complex problems, instead of making use of a much larger set of stakeholders that undoubtedly was relevant to the situation.

For each stakeholder, a list of assumptions is developed. What would have to be true about any and all aspects of each stakeholder in order to provide maximum support for the conclusion? Each assumption is stated in a form intended to maximize this support, no matter how obvious or, alternatively, how ridiculous the assumption may seem. The "truth" of each assumption will be investigated later.

In order to argue that "we can apply to our jobs what we learn in these workshops," for the boss as the stakeholder, the relevant C-group usually uncovers these supporting assumptions: Our boss is eager to do things in new ways; she understands the methods and has acquired the necessary skills to use the methods effectively; she will encourage us to apply what we learn; she will make sure that all the members of our work group pressure one another to apply the new skills; the culture of our work group supports doing things in new ways, taking risks, and learning from mistakes.

In order to argue that "this organization can be successful if each manager vows to do his very best," for the person as a stakeholder, the relevant C-group usually uncovers these supporting assumptions: Commitment to do something differently is the same as actually doing it; each person is in complete control of his or her destiny in the organization; the organization is the sum of its people—nothing more, nothing less; other people in the organization do not influence what each of us does; the formal documents, such as the reward system, do not influence what we do; if there is a culture in the organization or in our work groups, it does not influence how we behave.

Now, perhaps for the first time, the managers come face to face with their unstated assumptions about planned change—what it takes to change behavior in a complex organization. Just as they were pleased to see their actual norms of behavior exposed for the first time during the culture track, the managers also show signs of delight as they learn to uncover one more barrier to organizational success.

### Classifying Assumptions

Are all assumptions of equal importance? It seems there are always tangential assumptions that, even if they are false, do not prevent one from arguing strongly for the same conclusion. But there may be one or more assumptions that, if they indeed turn out to be false, would greatly undermine one's entire argument. In this case, one can no longer argue for the conclusion when the fallacy of such a basic assumption has been revealed. The assumption that "the consumer does not understand the workshop material," for example, may be unimportant so long as the consumer receives quality service on a timely basis. But the assumption that "we can learn the skills well enough to apply them to real problems" is crucial to the argument that the managers can apply to their jobs what they learn in the workshop.

Are all assumptions equally credible? It seems that some

assumptions are more certain (or uncertain) than others. On the one hand, a *fact* is an assumption that is believed to be true—or false— with complete certainty. On the other hand, an assumption has great uncertainty when no one in the organization can predict or control its eventual outcome. The assumption that "our boss will encourage us to apply what we learn" may be rather uncertain. But the assumption that "we can teach our subordinates the basic concepts of the management skills track" may be more certain, since each manager has the formal authority to set the meeting agendas for her own work group. And the assumption that "our subordinates can apply what we learned without our aid" is very certain to be *false*—but certain it is, nevertheless.

Just as the four C-groups are beginning to question whether it is possible to manage the tens, if not hundreds, of assumptions behind every conclusion, a scheme is offered for classifying— organizing and prioritizing—all their assumptions. Figure 12

**Figure 12. Assumption Matrix.**

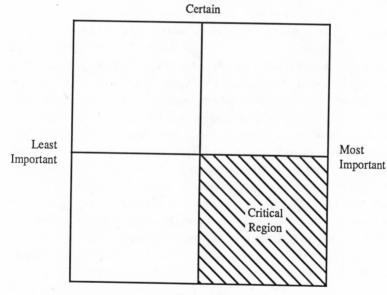

Certain

Least Important

Most Important

Critical Region

Uncertain

shows a matrix for plotting any assumption according to its importance to the initial conclusion as well as according to its uncertainty. Is the assumption, relatively speaking, most important to arguing for one's conclusion or is it least important? Is the assumption, as stated, fairly certain to be true, or is its truth uncertain? Combining these two dimensions for classifying assumptions results in four categories: (1) certain, least important, (2) certain, most important, (3) uncertain, least important, (4) uncertain, most important.

The first category (certain and least important assumptions) represents trivia—highly certain facts that have little bearing on the issue at hand. The second category (certain and most important assumptions) represents important facts; if we *know* them to be true, these assumptions do not reveal anything new. In this second category, however, it might be surprising to discover that some basic assumptions behind our favorite conclusions—now that these assumptions have been exposed for inspection—are clearly false, when all along we assumed just the opposite. The third category (uncertain and least important assumptions) shows what is not fully known to be true (or false), but these matters are not core to the arguments being presented. The fourth category (uncertain and most important assumptions) highlights the whole reason for classifying assumptions. Essentially, this fourth category displays assumptions that are most important to the group's arguments—if the group is wrong about these assumptions, its arguments will collapse—yet there is considerable uncertainty as to the truth or falsity of these assumptions. In fact, maximum uncertainty suggests a 50/50 proposition: The most important assumptions, as stated, are just as likely to be false as they are to be true.

The fourth category is referred to as the *critical region* for each C-group. This area is where the ultimate challenge to any argument will be directed. Too often, this critical region not only is ignored but is deliberately repressed. Individuals and groups arguing strongly for their positions do not want to expose their Achilles' heel: Others would see the weakness of their arguments. In short, building one's problem definition or implementation plan on assumptions in the critical region is like building one's house on a foundation of quicksand.

Each C-group is given felt pens and easel pads and asked to classify its assumptions according to the four cells of the matrix. Regarding the conclusion that "this organization can be successful without any change at all," for example, the assumptions that "no new competitors will enter our industry" and "our competitors will do in the future just as they have done in the past" would most likely be sorted into the critical region of the assumption matrix.

### Synthesizing Assumptions

After each C-group has prepared its matrix, all participants go to a community room for an intergroup challenge of assumptions. Each C-group is placed on the hot seat as the other groups have the opportunity, one by one, to question and challenge the focal group's assumption matrix. This debate, while very constructive, is very intense, due to the sharp personality differences across the four C-groups. Nevertheless, concessions are made during the debate as one or more groups realize they cannot get away with one or more assumptions that, upon inspection, do not seem very credible. Take, for example, the assumption that "the culture of the organization has no impact on what goes on." This assumption does not receive much support, especially since the culture track has already had a significant impact on each work group.

After a thorough debate has taken place on all the assumptions that were called into question, the time has come for each C-group to summarize the remaining issues that have not been resolved. These issues represent the differences that one or more groups cannot quite accept. Often these issues are the absolute core of the problem—the crucial assumptions that fall into the two most important regions of the matrix. There may be considerable disagreement as to the wording of these assumptions, whether a particular assumption is to be viewed as true or false, and how uncertain these assumptions really are. A typical unresolved issue concerns whether top management will support *and* apply the new ways of defining and solving problems—or are they merely giving lip service to the improvement program?

The focus next shifts to examining the unresolved issues that still divide the C-groups so that a complete synthesis of assumptions can be obtained. This synthesis cannot be accomplished by a single C-group, because each group is blinded by its own biases—reinforced by personality types and areas of expertise. Instead, a new group—a synthesis group—is formed by drawing together representatives from each of the original C-groups. If there are four C-groups, for example, two managers are appointed from each C-group to form an eight-person synthesis group (S-group).

As the S-group focuses on what all C-groups sorted into the two most important cells of the matrix (the right-hand side of Figure 12), it often is desirable to collect information from any source available (people, books, newspapers, scientific research) on the actual "truth" of these assumptions. This new information may place the assumptions in the certain region, although the assumptions may have to be stated differently according to what is learned. The advantage of removing assumptions from the critical region is that one can then argue for the conclusion with much more confidence. Consider, for example, the assumption that "the boss will support the use of assumptional analysis for defining problems before solutions are chosen." In this case, a few approaches can be explored to test the truth of this critical assumption—perhaps with the bosses themselves in a face-to-face meeting. Depending on what is discovered as a result of this inquiry, one or more assumptions may be reworded and reclassified.

The synthesized matrix, adjusted for new information, now becomes the foundation for deducing a new conclusion. In other words, what conclusion follows logically from all the assumptions as stated—particularly the assumptions in the two most important cells of the matrix? In using the transfer-of-learning problem to teach managers the skills for assumptional analysis, sometimes the new conclusion is twofold: (1) Managers *must* apply to their jobs what they learn in the workshops if they are serious about creating and maintaining organizational success, and (2) managers must *change*, wherever and whenever it is possible, the characteristics of stakeholders that do not contribute to organizational success. This new conclusion, particularly the second part, reveals altogether new alternative solutions (branches) on the new—hybrid—decision tree in the forest, as shown earlier by the dotted lines in Figure 10.

Apparently, in order to deduce this twofold conclusion, the

managers have learned that they do not have to regard their assumptions as fixed. Such a realization is rather ironic, since assumptions have been defined as the givens—as the noncontrollable features of internal and external stakeholders. Instead, as a result of having learned the three parts of assumptional analysis, the enlightened managers develop a very different assumption about the nature of assumptions: Assumptions change as stakeholders are changed. Any conclusion that is desired, with concerted action, can become true! In fact, managing the organization's internal stakeholders (superiors, peers, subordinates, groups, departments, divisions, board of directors) determines most of what takes place anyway, and even the external stakeholders can be influenced to some degree. After the workshops are finished, it is the resourceful managers who proceed to organize efforts that will influence all relevant stakeholders and, thereby, take the necessary responsibility—the *internal* control and commitment—to improve their organizations.

## The Bottom Line

As managers are learning the skills for problem management and assumptional analysis, they become more and more eager to apply these skills to real problems and not just to workshop exercises. The managers now recognize the various errors they have made in the past: sensing errors, defining errors, solving errors, and implementing errors. They vow to search out people with different personalities and areas of expertise in order to include them in group discussions on defining problems and implementing solutions. The managers also realize that only by bringing assumptions out into the open for a thorough and systematic examination will they be able to manage dynamic complexity. Thoughtfully, but deliberately, the managers enter their new holographic world.

# 5

# The Team-Building Track:
## Infusing New Cultures and Skills Throughout the Organization

The strong manager capable of almost single-handedly turning around an organization or department, while still a folk hero in the eyes of many, has given way to the recent demands of increasingly complex systems for managers who are able to pull together people of diverse backgrounds, personalities, training, and experience and weld them into an effective working group. This modern manager has shifted from dealing with problems on a one-on-one basis to solving more problems collectively, involving everyone who has a contribution to make in either solving a problem or implementing actions. In this context, the manager is a coach, a facilitator, a developer, a team builder.

—Dyer, 1977, p. xi

The culture track emphasizes how each work group must pressure its members toward more effective behavior and attitudes on the job. The management skills track emphasizes how all newly acquired skills for problem management and assumptional analysis must be transferred from the classroom to the job. Now we will see how the team-building track completes what these earlier tracks started: Team building fully activates both the new culture and the new skills throughout the entire organization.

The transition from classroom to workplace is not an easy one, either for those managers who are most familiar with an autocratic style of leadership or for those subordinates who prefer to play it safe. Even though all managers have learned that only a participative approach can hope to bring forth the necessary information and expertise to manage complex problems, adopting a participative style is exceedingly hard for autocratic leaders. Similarly, even though all members have learned the importance of behaving according to the new cultural norms that foster trust, communication, and information sharing, asserting one's viewpoints or disagreeing with the boss in public is a frightening experience for reticent employees. During the first two tracks, superiors and subordinates have been deliberately separated from each other during all workshop activities. Consequently, neither has fully confirmed the legitimacy of any behavior change directly to the other. Thus it is natural for them to fall back to their old ways of functioning in the organization, regardless of all the pressure to change.

By officially reuniting the superiors and subordinates in their work groups for the team-building track, however, the new roles of leader and follower become legitimized in face-to-face work group meetings. The only leadership style that will be considered acceptable for managing complex problems is participative management. Similarly, the only followership style that will be considered acceptable is one that provides all the relevant contributions for all group discussions. It is during the team-building track that the pressure to change becomes overwhelming for anyone, whether boss or subordinate, who still behaves according to traditional practices.

This chapter is organized into three approaches for fostering successful problem management on the job: managing troublemakers, team building, and interteam building. The first approach considers how to manage the tough problems created by troublemakers—persons whose behavior severely restricts the development of trust and cooperation in the organization. Once the troublemakers are put in check, attention focuses on developing each work group into an effective team by applying both the new culture and the new skills for problem management. Lastly, once each work group is a well-functioning team, the third approach, interteam building, addresses the special problems created by interconnected groups that compete with each other for resources, power, and glory. As a result, uncooperative cliques gradually become cooperative teams.

## Managing Troublemakers

Just how badly can people behave? What happens when their deepest animal instincts and their most aggressive fantasies go unchecked? What behavior is possible when the culture and the system of organization do not curtail people's dark side? Building on accounts given by Colin Turnbull—an anthropologist with the American Museum of Natural History—Allen (1980, pp. 27-28) vividly depicts the epitome of horrendous behavior by a tribe known as the Ik:

> It is hard to imagine a group of people more selfish and ruthlessly cruel than the Ik, a small tribe of nomadic hunters who were living out their lives in a remote region of East Africa in the early 1960s. They were not only unkind, but heartless; not only stingy, but maliciously grasping; not only dishonest, but cunningly deceitful. They were selfish and ruthlessly cruel beyond the imagination. They pushed their children out of the home at three years of age to fend for themselves—and then stole food from them. They stole from the elderly, the weak, the blind. The strongest men grabbed the limited food supply for themselves. When they found game in the fields, they ate it on the spot instead of taking some home to their starving families. They even ate it raw, for fear the smoke might attract others and force them to share. It was common for a brother to take food from the hand of a sick brother, to turn a sick family member out of the house to die. Even the last of the ritual priests was abandoned by his son and sent out to his death. Old people were frequently left alone in their huts to die.

Sometimes they were pushed off the sides of the mountain to the amusement of other tribesmen, and once, when a blind woman fell off a cliff and landed on her back like a tortoise, helpless with all four limbs flailing the air, the others went into peals of laughter and left her struggling. The killing of a child by a leopard was seen as a cause for celebration—it meant that there was edible game nearby. The people went out, found the leopard, ate both it and the child on the spot.

Allen (1980, p. 28) recognizes that the behavior of the Ik is not restricted to East Africa but can be witnessed in any organization:

With very little effort of the imagination, we can discover the Ik in the office, in the classroom, in the committee and boardroom, everywhere demonstrating just how badly it is possible for people to behave. There is the pusher, the grabber, the stealer, the nonsharer, the one who abandons, the one who laughs at others' struggles, the one who hides his riches for fear that they will be taken from him, and the one who risks the lives of others to add to his own wealth.

Troublemakers come in many varieties. Bramson (1981), in his book *Coping with Difficult People*, profiles some of these characters as Sherman tanks, snipers, exploders, and bulldozers. It does not take much imagination to picture these types in action or to identify people we know who fit these types almost to a T. Similarly, Lombardo and McCall (1984, p. 45), in an article titled "The Intolerable Boss," show how some bosses—described variously as snakes-in-the-grass, Attilas, heel grinders, egotists, dodgers, and detail drones—torment their subordinates:

He was a living snake and a pathological liar. His decisions were based on whoever talked to him last. He was a little dictator. . . . If anyone else tried to make a decision, he took it as a personal insult.

Does this sound like anyone you know—your current boss, perhaps, or one you've endured in the past? Most people have met up with at least one impossible boss—someone who fully deserved unflattering characterizations like the ones above.

In a *Fortune* article titled "The Ten Toughest Bosses in America," Flax (1984, pp. 18–23) summarizes comments made by subordinates about their tough bosses:

Working for him is like a war. A lot of people get shot up; the survivors go on to the next battle. . . . Comes across as being a Napoleon complex—he has to throw his weight around. . . . Unwilling to entertain ideas that don't fit with his. . . . Employees are scared to death of him. . . . Wild temper tantrums and firing threats commonplace.

It would take too much space to provide a full account of each type of troublemaker and the psychodynamics that make these people the way they are. Suffice it to say that deep within each type is an insecure and troubled person, one who copes with his inner conflicts and negative self-image by projecting them onto other people. In essence, troublemakers spend most of their energy surviving, defending, protecting, and living out their problems on others. There is a stark intensity in this life-and-death struggle with the world. And make no mistake about it, troubled persons are very much at war—they have no inner peace.

For some types of troublemakers, there is a dire need to control everything and everyone in every situation. No matter how much power and authority such a person may have, it still is not enough. The need is insatiable. For other types who have grown up in an atmosphere of suspicion, insufficient love, and constant disappointment, there is an extraordinary mistrust of others in everything they do. Such people demand blind loyalty and complete harmony—anything less is taken as a personal affront. Still other types must win every dispute at any cost and must receive all the credit for any success. Some of these troublemakers are especially aggressive and hostile toward organizational members as a way of getting back at people (mainly parents and "significant others") who inflicted great pain on them in the past.

Figure 13 summarizes the various coping styles that troublemakers use in order to satisfy three basic ego needs: achievement,

**Figure 13. Troublemaker Coping Styles.**

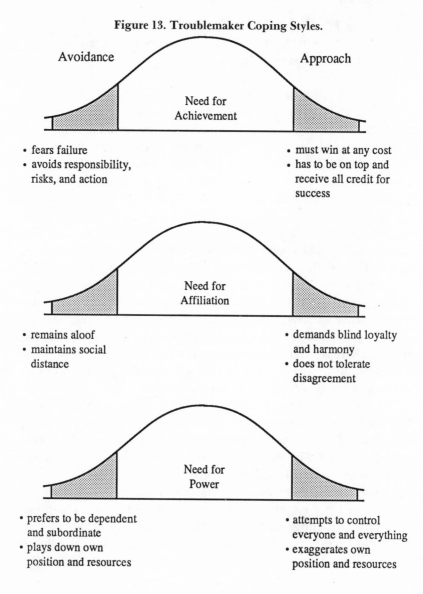

Avoidance                                              Approach

Need for
Achievement

• fears failure                                    • must win at any cost
• avoids responsibility,                           • has to be on top and
  risks, and action                                  receive all credit for
                                                     success

Need for
Affiliation

• remains aloof                                    • demands blind loyalty
• maintains social                                   and harmony
  distance                                         • does not tolerate
                                                     disagreement

Need for
Power

• prefers to be dependent                          • attempts to control
  and subordinate                                    everyone and everything
• plays down own                                   • exaggerates own
  position and resources                             position and resources

affiliation, and power (Atkinson, 1958). "Normal" people vary in the strength of their needs for competing with some standard of excellence, being accepted by coworkers, and controlling the means of influencing others—as illustrated by the open areas under each of the three normal distributions. Anyone who tries to satisfy his ego needs by approaching or avoiding behavior in a more extreme form, in spite of the needs of others, is likely to be viewed as a troublemaker. Thus, as shown by the shaded areas in each of the three distributions, troublemakers act out the extremes of avoidance or approach behavior in an intense and rigid manner. While the approach side may appear to represent the most disruptive coping styles that interfere with organizational success, a boss that acts out the avoidance side is disruptive for group members who are willing to take risks, work together, and influence one another.

The connection between how one was treated in years past and how one copes with the world today is evident with all the troublemakers. Thus if a person was shattered or abused in childhood (physically or psychologically), has never felt good about himself as a person (because he was taught to see himself as bad and guilty—how else can a child explain the abuse?), and has never acquired a sense of responsibility for his actions (the shame of doing one more thing wrong would be too much to bear), then becoming a troublemaker is a likely outcome.

If we understand these psychodynamics, it comes as no surprise that troublemakers are not likely to learn from reading self-awareness books, from observing how others seem to examine themselves and change for the better, and from attending the management skills track. More often than not, troublemakers attest to the great value of new material for all the *other* managers who desperately need to change. Troublemakers do not see that they themselves need to question their behavior and learn new management skills. They are too troubled to look inside, see what is there, and change it.

A completely integrated program for improving organizations encourages all members to question their habits, expose their cultural norms, examine their assumptions, learn new skills, and cooperate with others. How are troublemakers likely to react to these intrusions into *their* organization? How are they likely to interpret these efforts at learning and change? A troublemaker may very well interpret an improvement program as an act of war.

Understandably, some people feel that troublemakers should be managed at the *start* of the program. But I have learned that not until the program has been proceeding for several months is the organization really prepared to manage these troubled persons. Generally speaking, managers must have acquired effective skills for people management and must have developed a shared commitment to organizational success before they are able and willing to confront disruptive behavior. At the same time, all members must be encouraged to confront behavior that does not support the new cultural norms—which will only happen after the new sanctioning systems are put to use. Only when the organization is ready to address on-the-job problems with the new culture, new skills, *and* both bosses and subordinates present in the work groups is it ready to manage troublemakers. If the troublemakers are *not* confronted at this time, victimized members (and anyone else who knows of a troublemaker's abuse) quickly lose faith in the improvement program: "How can we take such a program seriously if it doesn't address the fear this organization inflicts on innocent members? How can top management excuse such psychological harassment while they claim to be improving things?"

Managing troublemakers involves finding out who they are and then counseling them to curb their disruptive behavior. Although troublemakers have a hard time receiving any kind of feedback, a face-to-face counseling session is the most direct way to convey the corporate message: Troublemaking behavior will no longer be tolerated in this organization. Because of the deep psychological conflicts that drive troublemakers to act in dysfunctional ways, a skilled consultant is needed to control these difficult people. Most managers have not acquired the skills to deal with pathology.

### Identifying Troublemakers

It is essential to distinguish between troublemakers (destructive individuals) and objectors (well-intentioned deviants). These two types should never be confused. Objectors, according to Ewing

(1983), are mentally healthy people who happen to disagree with some decision or action by those holding—or controlling—the majority view. The management skills track emphasizes the importance of listening to the deviants, since they are the ones who have the specialized knowledge for their piece of the whole problem. Overruling them may smooth conflicts but will quickly result in numerous errors in problem management, since examining differences is critical for solving complex problems.

In contrast, troublemakers are not well-intentioned deviants who simply express disagreement with some decision or action. Rather, troublemakers enact unhealthy and even destructive behavior, as displayed by the Ik: lying, cheating, stealing, harassing, intimidating, and deliberately hurting other people. When troublemakers are allowed to act out their destructive tendencies on others, it is nearly impossible to have a meaningful discussion on complex problems. They prevent both majority and minority views from being voiced, let alone heard.

Often the organization's troublemakers come to the attention of the consultants during the diagnostic stage of planned change (Chapter Two). While the interviews are being conducted, certain names are inevitably mentioned again and again. Stories are told of mean and hostile acts that have hurt other people or even the organization as a whole. While stories often are exaggerated, distorted by years of repetition, one must be careful not to discount them when told by many interviewees. In some cases, the stories are so alarming that even if they were only 10 percent true one would have to take such information seriously.

The consultants also become aware of troublemakers during the culture track and the management skills track. Since troublemakers are usually unaware of how their behavior affects those around them, they create trouble right in front of everyone— making hostile remarks that are not germane to the topic of conversation, showing anger in verbal and nonverbal ways, and discouraging others from taking the discussion seriously. As the earlier tracks proceed, several members may speak to the consultants about the difficulty of applying new learning back on the job. Their own managers ridicule them and even threaten them with bad performance reviews if they continue to attend the workshop meetings.

Identifying troublemakers is a more delicate process than it may seem. When there has been widespread intimidation on the part of a manager, his victims may be afraid to come forth and reveal injustices. Sometimes they are convinced that if the trouble-maker even suspects that others have revealed his name, he will take revenge. It is not uncommon for members to fear that this troublemaker will fire them for revealing anything to the consul-tants. Whether this is all due to fear or has some basis in reality is not clear. But it does cause members to hold back information on who is causing trouble for others. Ideally, as the team-building track proceeds these members will begin to draw attention to troublemaking behavior when they see others taking risks for organizational success.

The troublemakers may range from a few people to as many as a dozen for a large organization; every organization seems to have at least one such individual. Experience has shown that the great majority of troublemakers are in management positions throughout the hierarchy where they exploit formal authority to their full advantage. Occasionally, however, nonmanagement personnel rely on their technical expertise or their informal ringleader status in order to get away with disruptive behavior.

### Counseling Troublemakers

Each troublemaker is scheduled for a separate counseling session with a specially trained consultant. During this session, the consultant explains why the person was asked to attend. The consultant mentions the reported incidents and impressions (while protecting the confidentiality of the sources), emphasizing that these stories might be totally distorted. Any single incident can be explained away quite easily. But as a whole, as a pattern, is there any plausibility to these accounts? How can this person explain the perception others have of him or her?

Even though the person is shocked at being labeled a troublemaker, in rare cases he does seem to appreciate being given the information. After he recovers from the shock, he begins to explore how the incidents developed and how the perceptions must have formed. The individual then outlines how he plans to correct the perceptions, as well as his behavior. Here the person recognizes the problem and wants to solve it. Such an adaptive response suggests that he was mislabeled as a troublemaker—due to either abrasive behavior or embarrassing incidents. In these rare cases, perhaps no one has ever tried to tell him the problem and, consequently, he never has had the chance to change. But now this situation can be corrected.

In most cases, however, the troublemaker becomes defensive, argumentative, and nasty as the consultant tries to offer constructive, compassionate feedback. Should the consultant point out that the person's response seems to confirm what has just been described? If the troublemaker is extremely defensive, there is little likelihood that he will even hear the message. Instead, he will work very hard at protecting himself, as always. But the corporate message has been given, and the person has been put on the alert. The consultant concludes the meeting by encouraging the troublemaker to think about their discussion and indicating that there will be follow-up meetings to see how things are going.

Some troublemakers will act as if their behavior has changed, hoping that the consultants will leave shortly and that everything will go back to "normal." But a few weeks after the first meeting with each troublemaker, the consultant schedules the next round of counseling sessions to review what has transpired. Often, the same discussions are held again. The troublemaker insists that her behavior is fine—why can no one else see this? She claims that she is a victim of circumstance or of misunderstanding. She just does not see how her motives and behavior can be so misconstrued. Perhaps other members are simply jealous of her energy, intelligence, and accomplishments.

During these sessions, the consultants see creativity at work. The troublemakers can turn, rationalize, distort, and justify almost anything. These people, because of their wartime tactics, have learned to twist reality so that it matches the image they have of themselves. If the facts do not fit their needs, they change the facts. They come up with a new reality to explain the worth of their net contributions. The most vivid example of these distortions is illustrated by the troublemaker's insistence that she *likes* certain individuals—who just happen to be the very ones who have been hurt by her time and time again. Often these are the people who reported the troublemaker to the consultants in the first place. Such is the power of psychological compensation!

There may be as many as four to six counseling sessions over a period of several months in order to get each troublemaker to curb his or her disruptive behavior. It should be apparent, therefore, why top management's support must be behind such a confrontation. Without this support, the troublemakers will not show up for their counseling sessions and will ignore all the related discussions. Without this support, members will not confront the troublemakers for fear of reprisal. But if everyone is told in no uncertain terms that disruptive behavior will not be tolerated, the message will be received.

### Team Building

The purpose of team building is to help each work group use *all* its information and expertise in managing complex problems. Each work group must learn how to establish an effective process for all group discussions, based on all the material learned in the prior tracks: At the start of each meeting, group members should plan their time wisely and determine the priority of all agenda items before they discuss any item at length. They agree to address the most important items first and the less important items last. Group members also should plan how each agenda item will be approached and whether it can be subdivided into manageable parts, so that dynamic complexity does not immobilize them. Spending a little time planning these matters *before* proceeding usually saves a lot of time later. Once the plan is developed, the assumptions underlying all subsequent discussions should be examined—not only to minimize the likelihood of committing problem management errors but also to cut down on the number of circular, repetitive, and superficial discussions.

Furthermore, the extroverts should make a special effort to bring the more introverted members into every discussion to ensure that all viewpoints are heard. Certainly, the dialogue should not be dominated by the talkative ones. Group members should regularly assess whether the group's culture continues to support new, bizarre, and provocative ideas. All communications should be courteous—respecting everyone's ego and treating everyone with dignity. Only one person in the group should be talking at one time and everyone else should be listening. The spirit should be collaborative (to join all ideas in a creative way for the best *group* outcome) and not competitive (to see who talks the most and who wins the final argument). Every now and then, members should halt the group discussion on content and inquire about the *process:* How are we doing as a group? Are we applying the new culture and the new skills we learned? If not, what should we be doing differently?

When every group meeting on complex problems reflects such an effective group process, each work group becomes a well-functioning team. If a stranger were to observe such a team in session, he would not be able to discern who is the superior and who are the subordinates. *Every* member would be contributing information and expertise as needed: Status distinctions and other irrelevant criteria would not be influencing the way in which important issues were being addressed and then resolved. The physical arrangement of the team would most likely be round—holistic—reflecting the equal opportunity that every member would have to participate in all discussions. Prior to team building (and especially before the start of the program), this same stranger would not have had any difficulty in correctly identifying the boss during any of the group's meetings: The boss would have been initiating, talking, directing, deciding, and concluding—more than anyone else, on every topic. In some cases, in fact, the boss would have been sitting at the end of a large rectangular table, in a very comfortable leather chair, dictating his pronouncements to his passive subordinates.

While these contrasting portrayals of group process may seem too simplistic and extreme, they nevertheless do capture the kind of transformation that begins during the first two tracks and concludes during the team-building track. (In the strategy-structure and reward system tracks, it is the egalitarian group process that will ensure that relevant expertise and information will be the primary ingredients used for reshaping the organization's formally documented systems—rather than the highest position, largest chair, or loudest voice.) Before the team-building track, for example, managers may have said: "I am willing to change so long as I don't have to do anything differently!" As team building proceeds, however, they begin to experience considerable social pressure to change their *behavior* and not just their words. Now one hears: "There is so much pressure to change—from our peers, from our superiors, from the consultants, and from ourselves." "I had no idea that my subordinates would take me to task if I didn't apply the basic principles of time management at every group meeting. They really expect me to use what we learned in the workshops." "In the past, we all tacitly agreed to give lip service to one improvement program after another: We knew instinctively that nothing of significance would ever change around here if all we did was to keep talking about it. Now there is more pain if we *don't* change behavior than if we do!"

There are five steps of team building: (1) reuniting the work group, (2) sensing and defining work group problems, (3) deriving solutions and developing action plans, (4) implementing action plans, and (5) monitoring and evaluating outcomes. Not surprisingly, the five steps of team building parallel quite closely the five steps of problem management. Indeed, team building *is* problem management applied to every work group in the organization. The issue is always the same: discovering what is wrong, doing something about it, and then finding out if the solution worked— and, if it did not, trying again.

### Step One: Reuniting the Work Group

In an on-site work facility, the bosses and their subordinates are brought together in their natural work groups for the first time during the improvement program. Since most work groups range in size from three to fifteen members, the consultant or facilitator can handle numerous groups in one session so long as the total number of persons is manageable. Furthermore, just as with the earlier tracks, these formal team-building sessions will be conducted at least every other month—and they will be supplemented by regular on-the-job work group meetings in which group process issues are placed on the formal agenda. Both the on-site team-building sessions and the on-the-job work group discussions provide the *working* environment to complete what the earlier tracks began in a *learning* environment.

Since virtually every manager is a member of two groups— the one in which he is the boss and the one in which he reports to his superior—many managers may have to do team building in *two* groups. If most of a manager's time is devoted to just one of these groups, however, he only needs to participate in that primary work group throughout the team-building track.

The first topic for team building focuses on the work done in the culture track. Since the superiors and subordinates were separated into their peer groups, each community may have developed different desired norms as well as different sanctioning systems to enforce the new norms. Now that the work group is intact, it is essential to develop a common approach to the culture track. Usually, it does not take much effort to resolve cultural differences and to integrate the two sanctioning systems into one. After all, both superiors and subordinates generally have experienced similar problems in the same work group. Thereafter, any further work on the culture track takes place in the combined team.

The second topic for team building focuses on the work done in the management skills track. Since only the managers have received formal skill training in people management, problem management, and assumptional analysis, each manager is asked to teach the new concepts and skills to those subordinates who did not attend the management skills workshops. For example, it is customary for each work group to profile its Jungian personality types for subsequent use during the steps of problem management. This means that nonsupervisory personnel now have their own personalities assessed by the Myers-Briggs Type Indicator (Myers, 1962) as was done for the managers in the previous track. If many managers perform this new teaching role effectively, the knowledge gained in previous workshops spreads far beyond those who participated directly. This new educational system, incidentally, also encourages the spread of *all* relevant knowledge and expertise throughout the organization.

*Step Two: Sensing and Defining Work Group Problems*

In a separate room, each work group answers the following questions. Sometimes it is useful to have each member answer these questions individually before the group discusses them:

1.   What is the group's mission? What are the group's objectives?
2.   How well is the group accomplishing its mission and objectives?
3.   What helps the group in performing its tasks?
4.   What hinders the group in performing its tasks?
5.   Are group members spending the right amount of time on the right tasks with the right objectives in mind?
6.   Do group members feel that their time is not being spent in the most productive way? How is their time being diverted?
7.   Do group members feel that all their expertise and experience are being used? How could their talent be used more productively?
8.   Are all problems brought out in the open so they can be addressed with *full* information and expertise? Why are some problems being avoided?
9.   How does the group's profile of personality types affect the five steps of problem management?
10.  Which steps of problem management does the group overemphasize? Which do they underemphasize? Which errors of problem management occur most frequently?

Either the manager or one of the group members summarizes the various responses to the ten questions on a flip pad for all group members to see. Sometimes it helps to divide the group's responses into two categories by making use of Lewin's (1951) force field analysis—still one of the basic tools for problem diagnosis. Responses are divided into driving forces and restraining forces. The former describe what is moving the group forward and the latter describe what is holding it back. The group's equilibrium can be altered by either enhancing the driving forces (doing even better what the group already does well) or reducing the restraining forces (removing the barriers to success).

As the important questions about work group functioning are first answered and then categorized, information that penetrates the inner workings of the group becomes available—important problems are sensed by group members. Problem definitions can be formulated by the methods of problem management. If any response to the ten questions suggests a simple problem, group consensus is sufficient to resolve any differences. (Simple problems only have one decision tree.) The group's need for clarification and documentation of work procedures, for example, could be handled easily in this manner. Alternatively, if any of the responses to the ten questions suggest a complex problem—such as establishing why the group's support services are not used more extensively throughout the organization—the more elaborate methods for problem management should be applied. Perhaps an assumptional analysis can be done by forming several subgroups to debate and then synthesize the underlying assumptions of each problem definition. Each subgroup can be composed of different personality types (STs, NTs, SFs, and NFs) in order to produce radically different perspectives—and, hence, different decision trees. This arrangement enables the whole work group to define its problems correctly before deriving and implementing solutions.

The responses to the ten questions may also suggest problems that not only are complex but have ramifications beyond the group's boundaries. Even conducting assumptional analysis within the group would be insufficient in this situation: The full range of expertise and information needed to define the problem would not be forthcoming in the analysis, since it resides in other groups in the organization. The problems that fit this type would be postponed until the interteam building is ready to be undertaken. Each work group, for now, does the best job it can in defining both the simple and complex problems that fall under its own jurisdiction.

### Step Three: Deriving Solutions and Developing Action Plans

A lively discussion unfolds when members consider what can be done to solve their group's problems—to derive solutions that either enhance the driving forces or reduce the restraining forces. Some of their exuberance stems from the prospect of managing their own problems, whereas in the past the members were controlled by their habit of not examining how their group functioned. The only topics that were covered previously were specific problems of a technical and business nature—not group process.

Since deriving solutions is considered a relatively simple task once the problem has been defined, group consensus is sufficient for selecting the solutions to implement. Perhaps a qualitative cost-benefit analysis can be performed to aid in choosing solutions. Developing action plans for implementing solutions, however, constitutes a more complex problem. Special care should be taken to learn if the work group understands the full context of implementation. Perhaps an assumptional analysis can be done to surface the various assumptions being made: the availability of resources, how other groups will react to the contemplated changes, and how top management will respond—in short, any assumption about any relevant internal or external stakeholder. Again, use can be made of the group's different personality types as an aid to creating and debating different decision trees.

When the important and uncertain assumptions have been identified (the critical region), the work group should collect more information about the validity of these assumptions before any action is taken. For example, will other groups provide the necessary support to implement the action plans? Knowing such information would make uncertain assumptions more certain. The work group would then be implementing its solutions based on the most accurate knowledge about all stakeholders.

### Step Four: Implementing Action Plans

A useful approach to implementation is to form several subgroups of two to five members and give each subgroup responsibility for implementing one or more of the action plans. A group of fifteen members may take the five plans, for example, and assign them to five subgroups. Either the manager or a group member can coordinate this distribution of assignments. As implementation proceeds, each subgroup should report back to the entire group often so that everyone knows what the other subgroups are doing and has an opportunity to offer suggestions and advice.

Naturally, the initial plans will need to be modified as more is learned about the critical assumptions made about each stakeholder. The subgroups, as well as the whole work group, may find it necessary to brainstorm about new ways to enhance the implementation of their action plans. Enough time should be devoted to each work group meeting so that the topic of group process is given sufficient attention.

### Step Five: Monitoring and Evaluating Outcomes

The last step of team building is assessing the outcomes of all the prior steps to see if the defined problems have been resolved. If not, then each step is examined and the necessary adjustments are made before any step is conducted again. And if new problems emerged during the preceding cycle of problem management, they are addressed in subsequent cycles.

When it comes to monitoring and evaluating outcomes, I have found that it is most beneficial to appoint one member as a "process observer" at the start of every group meeting. This person is responsible for monitoring how well the new culture and the new skills guide all group discussions. At the end of each meeting, he or she summarizes what the group did particularly well and in what ways the group fell short. Moreover, a different member should be appointed to this role every time the group meets. As a result, over a period of a few months, every member will have the opportunity to develop observation skills and practice giving constructive feedback. Eventually, it will no longer be necessary to appoint a formal process observer—the responsibility for assessing and improving the group's process will have become shared among all group members. If each group is required to make use of rotating process observers during the first few months of the team-building track, it is virtually guaranteed that the new culture and the new skills will be used at all times.

### Interteam Building

Team building works on single parts of the whole organization, one at a time. *Interteam* building is necessary because these parts do not make up a mechanical system. Rather, the parts of the organization are strongly interconnected at the surface (task assignments) and below the surface (cultural norms), which makes for a complex hologram. A group may not be able to begin its tasks until it receives certain inputs from another group (information, materials, designs, resources), and the value of the group's contributions may be affected by how well its output is actually utilized by some other group (intermediate services or products). Even if each work group were independent in a task sense, each group would have to be isolated from the others to be independent in a cultural sense. Members from one group observe and interact with members of other groups. They compare, compete, help, and hurt one another. The objective of interteam building is to promote the most functional relationships among groups.

To convey how the three processes of managing troublemakers, team building, and interteam building must be conducted in sequence, Figure 14 illustrates their three focal points: troublemakers (represented as solid circles), team building (the larger circles around each box), and interteam building (the double arrows between teams). Just as the troublemakers must be managed before significant progress can be expected with team building, sufficient progress with each team-building effort is necessary before an interteam effort should begin. How can one resolve the problems that divide two or more groups if the groups themselves are unable to discuss their own behavior? Unless team building has already been successful, interteam building will result in finger pointing, scapegoating, and disruptive behavior. Just as troublemakers tend to project their internal conflicts onto others, emotionally torn groups project their mistrust and suspicion onto other groups in the organization. Groups can become cliques fighting over the same issues that troublemakers fight over—except that a group is a much more powerful force than one person.

Often, intergroup problems are pinpointed when the separate groups begin their team-building sessions. As solutions and action plans are being developed, each group delays discussion of these problems until its internal functioning has improved. Now, however, one group can invite other groups to explore their

Figure 14. Team Building.

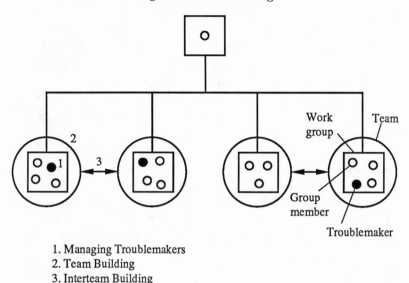

1. Managing Troublemakers
2. Team Building
3. Interteam Building

intergroup problems (assuming that these other groups are ready to step beyond their own borders).

The five steps of interteam building exactly parallel the five steps of team building applied to each work group. Since this chapter already has elaborated on these steps, the following discussion covers only those aspects of the process that are unique to defining and solving problems that stem from interconnected work groups. Note that every step of interteam building can proceed with or without consultants, depending on the managers' willingness and ability to be facilitators rather than bosses.

A manageable number of interdependent groups—those that are able and willing to address their mutual problems—are assembled for a one-day or two-day work session. Each group meets in a separate room to prepare a different list of *perceptions* for every other group attending the session. The members in each group list (1) their perceptions of the other groups' mission, objectives, and responsibilities, (2) their "gut image" of the other groups, and (3) their expectations of how the other groups see them. If there are four groups attending the workshop, each group prepares three such lists, one for each of the other groups (Blake, Mouton, and Sloma, 1965).

When the lists have been completed (usually in one to three hours, depending on the number of groups involved), all the groups meet back in a community room. One by one, each group makes a formal presentation of its lists to the other groups. Only questions of clarification should be allowed at this time. But all groups are encouraged to take extensive notes in order to prepare for the intergroup discussions a little later in the process.

The groups then meet back in their separate rooms. There the members review their notes, analyze what they have discovered, and determine what they wish to discuss with the other groups. Several revelations emerge during this discussion. The first revelation occurs when group members realize, often for the first time, the range of vastly different perceptions concerning the work domain of every group. Presumably, each group is guided by some formally documented charter, but this charter may be completely out of date. Often responsibilities have been established informally, often implicitly, based on the history of critical incidents among the groups. As a result, these conventional understandings are subject to selective memory and other perceptual distortions—depending on which group is questioned. This may seem obvious to the casual observer. To the groups, however, the *recognition* of these differences becomes a significant discovery.

The second revelation occurs when each group learns of its image within the other groups. I have found that revealing "gut images" is often a powerful experience. While group members can rationalize different perceptions of work domains rather easily, it is tougher to justify their image as empire builders, know-it-alls, kamikazes, disrupters, beggars, sinners, misers, or tightwads. Indeed, such images convey a strong emotional message that cannot be justified rationally. Rather, each group must come to terms with its style of relating to the other groups in the organization. Does its image help or hurt its own mission and objectives, let alone those of the whole organization?

The third revelation emerges from responses to the last item on the list: expectations. A comparison can be made between each group's explicit expectations of how it would be seen and how it actually was seen by the others. This comparison can be rather surprising. One group may have expected other groups to see it as productive, hardworking, and helpful to others. But the other groups may see this group as working hard only on the fun projects and being helpful only for certain "favored" groups—and then only when this is to its immediate advantage. Here the group has to examine why it might have made such poor predictions in judging its public image. Perhaps the group has a glorified vision of itself based on how it *wants* to be seen rather than how it really works with other groups.

All groups then meet back in a community room to discuss these findings in an open forum. Many new insights emerge from such in-depth exchanges. Since both the culture track and the management skills track have made significant progress (otherwise the team-building track would not have been initiated), one can expect minimum defensiveness among all the participants as the intensive discussions proceed. Even if a number of problems do not get defined in this first work session, at least everything is brought out in the open. After a few hours, the members summarize the key points that still divide the groups—the intergroup problems that get in the way of interteam cooperation.

If some problems appear to be very complex—such as reinterpreting group charters and mission statements—the methods of assumptional analysis again come in handy. Here are some examples of "initial" conclusions that help to get the process started: Continue to see each group as an island; shift to emphasizing intergroup cooperation and shared resources; disband all the groups and form entirely new ones. Since the focus is on interteam building, subgroups that form around initial problem definitions should consist of members from several different work groups. It is important to make sure that the very problems that were created by current group boundaries do not get in the way of solving the problems.

Either in the same work session or in a subsequent meeting, a community discussion is held to derive solutions and formulate action plans in order to resolve the problems. If the action plans and the methods of implementing them match the identified problems, and if sufficient time and energy have been devoted to these intergroup activities, considerable progress should have been made. Naturally, a number of errors in defining problems and in deriving and implementing solutions may have occurred. If necessary, the process of interteam building may have to be cycled through problem management again.

Littlejohn (1982, pp. 23–24, 28) provides a fitting summary of the benefits derived from most team-building efforts:

> Employees tend to develop a caring and sharing attitude. Mutual trust and support are fostered. Consequently, conflicts within the team can more easily be dealt with openly and constructively. Prior to introduction of the team concept, sensitive issues often lie hidden and are not discussed. After teams are formed, however, a healthy, constructive atmosphere for conflict resolution develops.
>
> Team members become better problem solvers, thanks to greater communication and mutual team support. Creativity and innovation can be expected to permeate the team interaction. As the team develops and grows, it becomes more cooperative and reflects greater coordination. Ultimately, productivity is significantly increased through the team's synergism. A collective strength is formed that is far superior to the sum of individual strengths, enabling the individual within a team to grow and produce. . . .
>
> Team management is not magic nor a panacea for all management ills. However, it is a better way to manage. It is a common-sense approach of letting people improve their performance by improving the process they use.

### The Bottom Line

When the three aspects of the team-building track have had their impact on the organization, the overall quality of decision making and action taking will be improved. Once the troublemakers have curtailed their disruptive behavior, everyone will feel freer to take chances and express opinions. Once each work group has been developed into an effective team, its specific work-related problems will be managed more effectively than ever before. Once all interconnected groups become cooperative teams, complex organizational problems that cut across traditional group boundaries will be managed explicitly.

Even if the first three tracks are entirely successful, the formally documented systems will not yet have been improved. Only the informal agreements, understandings, and cultural norms will have been modified. Now, however, the organization is ready to address the tough issues of its strategy-structure and reward system. We must make sure that all the members are working on the right tasks according to the right objectives and are rewarded properly for doing so.

# 6

## The Strategy-Structure Track:

### Realigning Objectives, Tasks, and People

> The structure of an organization is no longer viewed as a rigid definition of hierarchical levels and interrelationships among different groups. Managers use the organizational design process as a fundamental tool for implementing and communicating the strategic direction selected for the firm. . . . However, it should be recognized that strategy and structure are a two-way street, in which strategy is certainly influencing the resulting organizational design, but also the existing structure somehow constrains the strategic alternatives of the firm.
> —Hax and Majluf, 1983, pp. 72–73

The three most important questions confronting the members of an organization are: Where are we going? How will we get there? What will we receive for helping out? The answers to these questions must be developed in a systematic and thorough manner, since strategy, structure, and rewards have such a major impact on organizational success. Essentially, formal documents constitute the psychological contract between each individual and the organization concerning what behavior is expected and what behavior will be rewarded. While this contract is subject to negotiation and change, it is important to document it so that it can be understood and discussed. Otherwise, expectations and intentions—the

125

lifeblood of all human interaction—will be violated in a psychological sense, which will lead to unrealized aspirations in an organizational sense. In other words: If the strategy-structure and reward system are not established and documented properly, both the organization and its members will be misled.

This chapter presents the problem management organization (PMO) as an instrument to manage complex problems that affect the entire organization. In the present case, the PMO is used to realign the organization's strategy and structure. (In the next chapter, a new PMO is used to establish a performance-based reward system.) As we will see, the PMO is needed first to overcome the constraints that the current structure places on devising strategic alternatives. It is then needed to ensure an innovative and receptive environment for redistributing the organization's resources according to the new strategic plan. If the earlier tracks have not been managed properly, however, members will fight—overtly and covertly—to hold on to their fiefdoms and resources. The promise of organizational success will not be enough to motivate acceptance of a strategic-structural shift. Only if the firm has developed an adaptive culture, only if all its members have learned the skills for managing dynamic complexity, and only if a cooperative team spirit has been activated throughout the organization will the membership choose to realign its strategy and structure for the future.

### The Problem Management Organization

The PMO is an ideal way to assemble a diverse collection of members—from all areas and levels in the hierarchy—in order to manage organization-wide problems. This tool for problem management has been referred to as a parallel or collateral organization (Zand, 1981). The members in this unique arrangement spend two to ten hours a week working on complex problems; the rest of their time is spent back in the formal operational structure. Figure 15 shows the autonomy of, as well as the linkages between, the operational and the collateral structure. Both structures together form the problem management organization.

The major reason for using parallel structures with overlapping memberships in the PMO is to increase the likelihood that

**Figure 15. The Problem Management Organization.**

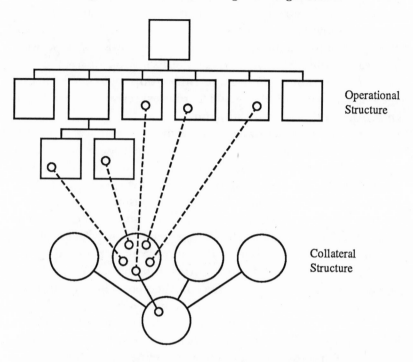

creative solutions to complex problems will be derived and implemented. A collateral structure encourages line managers to be directly involved in defining and solving complex problems; then, these same managers are directly responsible for implementing their solutions back in the operational structure—from a formal position of authority. And since all participants in the collateral structure are *required* to maintain extensive two-way communication with the rest of the membership, the PMO fosters organization-wide understanding of and commitment to all proposed solutions. The difficulty of assigning complex problems to staff groups, the customary practice, is that these groups are remote from the source of the problems, including the membership, and are not in a position of line authority to implement their own recommendations.

Thus the PMO fosters the ongoing cycle of sensing problems (in the operational structure), defining problems and deriving solutions (in the collateral structure), and implementing solutions and evaluating outcomes (back in the operational structure). As Figure 15 shows, the members in each collateral group come from different subunits in the operational structure—which suggests why interteam building often precedes the formation of a collateral structure. Without cooperative intergroup exchanges in the *operational* structure, one could hardly expect much sharing of knowledge in the collateral structure.

When the organization is ready to begin work on the complex problems of strategy and structure, the shadow track selects about twenty-five participants for the strategy-structure track. The shadow track, as discussed in Chapter Two, consists of top executives and other members who are responsible for implementing the whole improvement program. It uses these criteria for selection: The participants should represent all areas and levels in the organization involved in the improvement program; they should exemplify the desired norms and the use of problem management skills, as demonstrated by their behavior and attitudes at the workplace; they should be viewed by their peers and subordinates as formal and informal leaders—they should have clout. Ideally, when the rest of the membership sees the list of persons chosen to participate in the strategy-structure track, the response will be: "These are the right people to tackle our strategy-structure problems."

Once the participants in the strategy-structure track have been assembled for their first on-the-job work session, material on the topic of strategy and structure is presented and discussed. Sometimes consultants, external or internal, can teach participants the concepts they need to define and solve strategy-structure problems; other times, knowledgeable managers can provide the necessary methods. The goal is that all members in the strategy-structure track have a working knowledge of this dual problem (as discussed in the remainder of this chapter). Next, the participants review the diagnostic results that were presented by the consultants several months earlier. After having been exposed to the various theories and methods for determining a firm's direction and its organization of resources, the strategy-structure barriers to success that were noted become much more meaningful.

Following this first work session, the participants are prepared to address their organization's strategy-structure problems with all their knowledge and skills. And because of all the progress with the prior tracks, they will be especially sensitive to the dangers of committing problem management errors. They know that if a *defining* error is committed in either reshaping strategic directions or restructuring organizational resources, all subsequent efforts at implementing change will be wasted. But even if the right strategic plan and operational structure have been developed, the latent potential of the organization cannot be realized if an *implementing* error is committed. The other errors of problem management can spoil the overall success of the strategy-structure track, but it is the defining and implementing errors that are the most devastating to a problem management effort.

## From Assumptions to Strategies

A statement of strategy pinpoints the firm's direction much more precisely than a broad statement of vision, mission, or purpose. Strategy means choosing specific approaches for financing, producing, and marketing the firm's product or service—for example, *how* it plans to become the world-class leader in its chosen arena. Should the firm's sales outlets be franchised to independent retailers, or should it fully own and control the link between the organization and the customer? Should the firm's production facilities be upgraded to improve efficiency, or should it design and build completely new plants with new production technologies? Should the human resources department be training members for performing existing jobs, or should it be preparing members for the jobs of the future? Should R&D try to improve the quality of existing product lines, or should it be developing entirely new concepts for consumption? What *is* the competitive edge?

Deciding which combination of strategic choices to develop into one strategic plan is perhaps the most complex, far-reaching problem a firm can face. Just one mistake in any assumption about one stakeholder can lead to long-term trouble for an organization. It would take too much space to describe the full process by which participants in the strategy-structure track apply assumptional analysis to derive the right strategic plan. But it is useful to get a glimpse of the process through a hypothetical example. The case is the General Motors Company. The question is: What strategic plan should guide GM into the twenty-first century? This illustration is organized into three parts of assumptional analysis described in Chapter Four: surfacing strategic assumptions, classifying strategic assumptions, and synthesizing strategic assumptions.

### Surfacing Strategic Assumptions

O'Toole (1983, p. 4) discusses ten unchallenged assumptions that took General Motors into the 1970s:

1.  GM is in the business of making money, not cars.
2.  Success comes not from technological leadership but from having the resources to quickly adopt innovations successfully introduced by others.
3.  Cars are primarily status symbols. Styling is therefore more important than quality to buyers who are, after all, going to trade up every other year.
4.  The American car market is isolated from the rest of the world. Foreign competitors will never gain more than 15% of the domestic market.
5.  Energy will always be cheap and abundant.
6.  Workers do not have an important impact on productivity or product quality.
7.  The consumer movement does not represent the concerns of a significant portion [of] the American public.
8.  The government is the enemy. It must be fought tooth and nail every inch of the way.
9.  Strict, centralized financial controls are the secret to good administration.
10. Managers should be developed from the inside.

As we all know by now, the world changed drastically in the 1970s. Dynamic complexity caused these ten assumptions to become outdated—in fact wrong. Almost overnight, the very existence of one of the largest industrial corporations in the world was threatened as never before (O'Toole, 1983, p. 5):

> Gasoline became expensive; the auto market became internationalized; the rising cost of (and time required for) retooling made it necessary to be a leader rather than a follower in the introduction of new technology; consumer values changed from styling to quality; the size of families shrank; people could no longer afford to trade their cars in every few years; worker values and attitudes changed; successful government relations required cooperation rather than an adversarial relationship; the few "kooks" in California who bought Volkswagens and read *Consumer Reports* [became] an important segment of the auto buying public. . . . By 1980 the environment had changed so thoroughly that the brilliant assumptions created by the company's founders to meet the exigencies of the environment of the 1920s were inappropriate in the radically altered environment fifty years later.

How could one apply assumptional analysis to GM's problem of deriving a strategic plan for the twenty-first century? In order to mobilize the PMO, a diverse set of twenty-five people or so from all areas and levels in GM would be asked to participate in the strategy-structure track—selected from engineering, marketing, public relations, legal counsel, finance, new product development, manufacturing, human resources, and so on. These people, once gathered together, would produce some very different strategic alternatives: (1) Keep things the same. (2) Produce only economy cars. (3) Produce only big cars. (4) Shift to other modes of transportation. (5) Diversify into new markets. (6) Go out of business. While these alternatives as stated are extreme, such "initial" conclusions will bring out radically different assumptions beneath different decision trees in the complex strategic forest.

The twenty-five participants would sort themselves into six conclusion groups (C-groups) representing the six "initial" strategic conclusions. (This structure of C-groups represents the first row of groups in the collateral structure shown in Figure 15.) Next, each C-group would be asked to list all stakeholders, internal and external, relevant to its conclusion. The group arguing for "keep things the same," for example, might include the following stakeholders: the economy, the government, the consumer, the unions, competitors, stockholders, top management, and the rest of GM's members. This C-group would then list all the assumptions for each stakeholder that would have to be true in order to argue convincingly for its strategic conclusion. Most of these assumptions would be similar to GM's ten basic assumptions listed earlier: Foreign competition will stabilize; competitors will not provide technologically improved cars; the membership will continue to be satisfied working on the same cars in the same way; the unions will resist any strategic shift.

Another C-group, however, may suggest some *new* stakeholders and, as a result, some new assumptions. The group whose conclusion is "shift to other modes of transportation," for example, might list these stakeholders: the airline industry, the railroad industry, the inner-city rapid transport industry, companies providing alternative fuel sources, R&D organizations pursuing new technological breakthroughs, and the communications industry (as a substitute for transportation). Then assumptions about the properties and dynamics of these new stakeholders must be made explicit. Regarding the airline industry, this C-group would have to assume that short-range helicopter service (as further developed and supplied by airline companies) will substitute for automobiles in large urban areas (where the prime auto markets are located) in order to ease growing traffic, parking, and pollution problems.

### Classifying Strategic Assumptions

At this point in the process, each C-group must distinguish most important from least important assumptions and certain from uncertain assumptions. As before, assumptions that are both most important *and* uncertain are sorted into the critical region. Recall from the assumption matrix presented in Chapter Four (Figure 12) that any assumption sorted into this region is absolutely critical to the argument (if the assumption is wrong, it is impossible to argue for the conclusion), and yet there is considerable uncertainty with regard to its truth or falsity.

Regarding the least important versus most important distinction in the assumption matrix, the group arguing for "produce only big cars" would not be affected much by the assumption concerning *how* competitors will sell their cars in the world marketplace. This group's argument would be greatly affected, though, by assumptions concerning what consumers want and the availability of gasoline. If market research suggests that consumers will prefer high-quality fuel-efficient cars because they anticipate another worldwide energy crisis in the twenty-first century, this C-group will find it impossible to make a convincing argument for its initial conclusion.

Regarding the certain versus uncertain distinction in the assumption matrix, most Americans are absolutely sure that the United States government will not nationalize the automobile industry in the next ten years—or at least it is an assumption that is highly certain. Alternatively, believing that no competitor will introduce a major technological breakthrough in the auto industry in the next ten years is an assumption that is highly uncertain.

The C-group arguing for "shift to other modes of transportation" would put these assumptions in the critical region: What makes for success in one form of transportation leads to success in another (transportation is transportation); other auto firms will not follow this strategic move; shifting to different forms of transportation will provide more growth and profit opportunities than will be gained by remaining in the automobile industry.

### Synthesizing Strategic Assumptions

Once all the assumptions that underlie different decision trees have been debated by all six C-groups, attention focuses on synthesizing any unresolved issues into one assumption matrix. This synthesized assumption matrix will enable the participants to derive the best conclusion regarding GM's strategic plan for the twenty-first century. To proceed from unresolved issues to the "final" conclusion, two members from each C-group would be asked to form a synthesis group (S-group). (Figure 15, presented earlier, illustrates the transfer of members from each collateral group to the single synthesis group, shown at the very bottom of the collateral structure in the PMO.)

The S-group, in the hypothetical GM case, might recognize that several critical assumptions concern the wants and desires of the consumer. One C-group may have assumed that consumers want economy and quality, another C-group may have assumed that consumers want styling and comfort, and still another may have assumed that consumers are switching to other modes of transportation. Since all these assumptions fall into the uncertain and most important cell in the matrix—the critical region—it is essential to know the truth. The strength of all arguments and their corresponding conclusions rests on deciding what is an accurate assessment of consumer wants and needs. Perhaps additional market research can be undertaken to learn the validity of these critical assumptions.

It is fun to speculate what the final conclusion would be if GM really went through the three parts of assumptional analysis— so long as one realizes that speculation is no substitute for the actual process. When the realities of today's global marketplace have been reflected in all of GM's strategic and operating assumptions, the following strategic plan for the twenty-first century might be deduced.

First, GM would establish an automobile industrialization curve for every nation. This curve would show the decades when the highest growth potential for the sale of automobiles could be anticipated. Second, for these high-growth markets, GM would form joint ventures with their governments and other relevant organizations in order to develop the infrastructure needed to support automobile usage. Third, GM would concentrate its auto designing, manufacturing, and marketing efforts for these targeted Third World nations—as its assumptions warrant. Fourth, if and when the industrialization curve has passed the high growth potential for automobiles in a nation, GM would develop and supply alternative modes of personal transportation and get heavily involved in service. But since "transportation" seems distinctly different from "communication," GM would not enter this latter industry: GM would continue to move people instead of information.

When all the other participants in the strategy-structure track have endorsed the S-group's proposed strategic plan (after having made minor adjustments, as assumptions warrant), it is presented to GM's top management group. Any senior executive can make additional adjustments so long as they are justified by updated assumptions and new information—not by political pressure and vested interest. Once top management endorses the strategic plan (with the concurrence of the board of directors, if necessary), it is essential to document and distribute the new plan to all organizational members. In order to translate this strategic plan into organized action, however, GM would have to realign all its current resources with a new operational structure.

### From Strategies to Structures

What modifications in the operational structure are needed to implement a new strategic plan? And what impact will these modifications have on the organization's members? The more fundamental the change in strategic direction, the more pronounced will be the change in the operational structure and, therefore, the greater the effect on organizational members. If all the prior tracks have been conducted properly, however, the transition from one structural form to another can be accomplished with both imagination and compassion: Members *can* accept structural change if the process takes into account their wisdom and respects their dignity. Furthermore, just as the PMO can break the organization's tendency to see strategic alternatives only through the current structure of work units, now the PMO can be used to devise "initial" alternative conclusions and to implement a "final" operational structure. The process of transforming the new strategic plan into a new operational structure is described in three parts: operationalizing strategy, designing subunits, and implementing structure.

*Operationalizing Strategy*

If the organization's strategic potential is to be achieved, every member must be provided with an operational structure to guide his time and effort. I define organizational structure as (1) objectives to be pursued, (2) tasks to be performed, (3) the design of objectives and tasks into work units, and (4) the management hierarchy that coordinates all work units into a functioning whole. Making this structure *operational* means that the members who are assigned to work units must be given the resources—financial, technical, material, and informational—to translate plans into action.

Consider some examples of *objectives* to be pursued: to improve the financial return on investments; to obtain a leadership position in customer service; to increase the domestic market share; to penetrate new international markets; to lower the per-unit cost of production; to monitor all external stakeholders; to build an excellent working environment. These objectives are more specific than a strategic plan but not so specific that they indicate what has to be done in terms of tasks. Consider, now, some examples of *tasks* to be performed: designing new products; preparing annual budgets; conducting market surveys; planning technology studies; developing sales promotions; pricing new products; packing and shipping merchandise. These tasks are not so detailed as to describe minute-by-minute activities but are much more specific than the basic functions of finance, marketing, or engineering.

Figure 16 illustrates how strategy is operationalized throughout the organization: The topmost circle shows the full set of objectives, tasks, and people (including all other resources) that would be assigned to the president or whoever has chief responsibility for all that transpires. The next level breaks this total set of objectives, tasks, and people into divisions, defined as the broadest breakdown of the whole into its parts. Each of these divisions is responsible only for its assigned subset of objectives, tasks, and people. At the next level, each division, in turn, is divided into smaller, more manageable work units, each with an even more focused set of objectives, tasks, and people. These units may be departments or sections. Depending on the size of the organization,

Figure 16. Operationalizing Strategy.

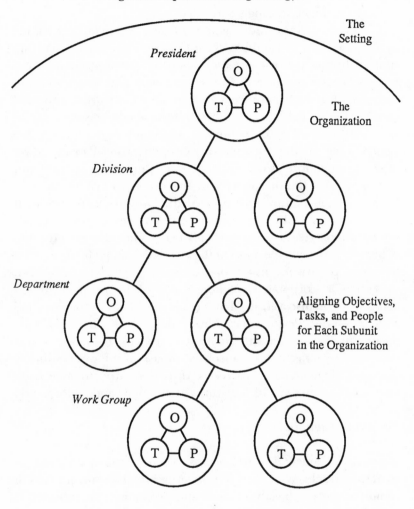

this process continues until the work group level is reached—here individual jobs are specified. The linkages that emerge from this level-by-level classification become the management hierarchy. Its purpose is to coordinate all the work that flows horizontally and vertically throughout the organization. For the sake of convenience, the term *subunit* will refer to a breakdown of the whole into its parts that usually implies a division but may just as well be a department or work group, depending on the focus.

Through various discussions in their collateral groups, the participants clearly see the powerful impact that operationalizing strategy has on performance and morale. If the strategic plan has not been translated correctly into specific objectives for the division (and then for the departments and then for the work groups and then for individual jobs), members' efforts would be steered in the wrong direction. In fact, errors in operationalizing strategy at the higher levels in the organization inevitably spread to the lower levels. Furthermore, if the objectives to be pursued in each subunit have not been linked correctly to the necessary tasks to be performed, members' time will be wasted as well. In other words: If objectives and tasks have not been documented properly, the organization's resources are probably being squandered. In the case of bureaucratic red tape, most of the members' time is being devoted to endless paperwork instead of getting the primary work done. In the case of a "corporate black hole," most of the members' time is being spent on discovering what is expected, what is important, and who is responsible for what. Thus either too much or too little documentation will result in misdirected efforts. Worse yet, if contradictory objectives and inconsistent tasks result from failing to operationalize strategy correctly into structure, members get frustrated and angry, which disturbs both morale and performance.

### Designing Subunits

A fundamental question must be addressed in the strategy-structure track: What are the criteria for determining which combinations of objectives, tasks, and people become subunits at each level in the hierarchy? Thompson's (1967) notion of task flows—how the performance of one task depends on the results of another—is exceedingly helpful in answering this question.

Thompson defines three types of task flow: pooled, sequential, and reciprocal. *Pooled* flows occur when two or more people can perform tasks independently of one another and then, at any time, the results can be added together to produce useful output—for example, three persons working on three unrelated projects, for three different clients, regularly combine their project revenues into corporate revenues. *Sequential* flows occur when a task must be completed by one person before another person can proceed with his or her assigned task in order to produce useful output—for example, a customer order must be recorded by a sales person before the item is removed from the shelf by a stockroom person, and only then can the item be mailed to the customer by someone in the shipping department. *Reciprocal* flows occur when frequent interactions and exchanges must take place among people in order to produce useful output—for example, designing a brand new product requires ongoing discussions among several persons in market research, engineering, and production. Figure 17 diagrams the three types of task flow, showing pooled flows as dotted lines, sequential flows as single arrows, and reciprocal flows as double arrows.

Thompson suggests that each type of task flow varies in the cost of managing it—which is determined primarily by the amount

**Figure 17. Three Types of Task Flow.**

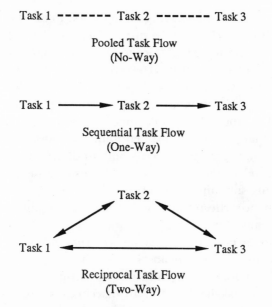

Task 1 ------- Task 2 ------- Task 3

Pooled Task Flow
(No-Way)

Task 1 ⟶ Task 2 ⟶ Task 3

Sequential Task Flow
(One-Way)

Task 2

Task 1 ⟷ Task 3

Reciprocal Task Flow
(Two-Way)

of time spent in coordinating related activities. Pooled flows are the least costly to manage simply because the outputs of different tasks can be combined rather quickly by simple rules and procedures. Sequential flows are more costly to manage than pooled flows, since more time for planning and scheduling is required to ensure the proper sequence of activity. Reciprocal flows are the most costly to manage, since considerable time is spent on back-and-forth adjustments among people as each one influences, and is influenced by, the other.

How can an operational structure be designed to minimize the cost of managing all the work? Thompson argues that the more costly task flows should be placed *within* subunits, while the less costly flows should be placed *between* subunits. Figure 18 illustrates the ideal case and the worst case for designing subunits. The ideal case shows that only pooled flows (dotted lines) are placed between subunits, while all sequential flows (single arrows) and reciprocal flows (double arrows) are placed within subunits. The worst case shows that reciprocal and sequential flows are placed between subunits, while only pooled flows are placed within subunits.

The closer an organization's subunits are to the ideal case, the lower the costs of managing all the work. In essence, coordinating task flows *within* a subunit is facilitated by the physical proximity of its members (face-to-face conversations), informal peer-group pressures (cultural sanctions), and the reward system that is administered primarily by the subunit's boss (formal sanctions). Coordinating task flows *between* subunit boundaries is obstructed by the considerable time it takes to reach people by phone or mail, to schedule intergroup meetings, and to reward some other manager's employees—both informally and formally.

To understand the full implications of different task flows for designing subunits, one must examine two related components of performance: effectiveness and efficiency. Organizational *effectiveness* means maximizing the chances for long-term survival by adapting to the needs of external and internal stakeholders. What is considered ineffective? Members may have developed the wrong strategic plan for the organization—resulting primarily from a limited set of stakeholders and an inaccurate set of assumptions. Organizational *efficiency* means maximizing the likelihood for

## Figure 18. Designing Subunits.

Correct Boundaries (Ideal Case)

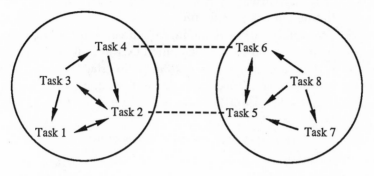

Incorrect Boundaries (Worst Case)

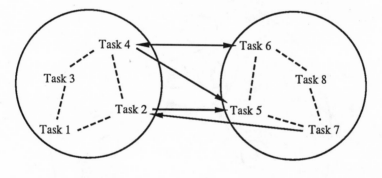

short-term productivity by working without wasting time, effort, or resources. What is considered inefficient? Members may (1) spend time on the wrong tasks—those that do not link to objectives, (2) not spend enough time on the right tasks—those that do link to objectives, and (3) be unable to work on the right tasks—those that have been assigned to some other subunit. It should be apparent that efficiency can be improved by shifting the time spent on the wrong tasks—or the wrong time spent on the right tasks—to the right time on the right tasks. Morale, incidentally, can be improved if members have the necessary strategy-structure linkages to work efficiently and effectively on their assigned jobs.

It is now possible to integrate most of the foregoing discussion on strategy, structure, efficiency, and effectiveness—through the mediating impact of subunits. Figure 19 shows how all the firm's documents (and corresponding resources) must be aligned at three interfaces—from the strategic interface through the structural interface to the job interface. The *strategic* interface considers how well the strategic plan has been derived for both external and internal stakeholders and has been translated into organizational

**Figure 19. Integrating Strategy and Structure.**

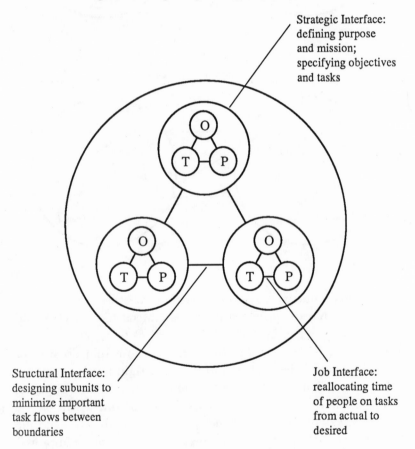

Strategic Interface: defining purpose and mission; specifying objectives and tasks

Structural Interface: designing subunits to minimize important task flows between boundaries

Job Interface: reallocating time of people on tasks from actual to desired objectives and tasks. The *structural* interface considers how well the troublesome task flows have been placed within rather than between subunits. The *job* interface considers how well subunit managers guide their subordinates to spend the right amount of time on the right tasks according to the right objectives.

If the strategic interface is not aligned properly, the remaining two interfaces are irrelevant. In this case, the structural interface is designing the wrong objectives, tasks, and people into subunits, which renders managers' efforts to align the job interface—the efficient allocation of members' time—inconsequential. Efficiency has no meaning if effectiveness is not being achieved. Alternatively, if the strategic interface is aligned properly (effective performance *can* be achieved) but the structural interface is not, the job interface still cannot be aligned for efficiency. Here members in each subunit are restricted in their efforts to perform well by the tasks they do not control. Lastly, even if both the strategic and structural interfaces are aligned properly, the subunit managers still must allocate their members' time on the right tasks with the right objectives if the job interface is to be aligned properly. But since managers now have the right objectives, tasks, and people under their authority, both effectiveness and efficiency can be achieved.

When the participants in the strategy-structure track discuss all the many implications of Figure 19 for their organization, they begin to sense the powerful impact that the design of subunits has had on performance and morale. Now they fully comprehend *why* a manager's biggest frustration is to be held responsible for a subunit's performance without having direct authority over all the vital tasks (and resources). These tasks, because of reciprocal and sequential task flows, are located in other subunits. Since the manager has no formal authority to tell other managers how to allocate their subordinates' time and effort, she has to "beg, borrow, or steal" so that these other subunits complete their work on time (or adjust what they are doing) so that her subunit can complete its job on time. Even after successful completion of the earlier tracks, sometimes as much as 80 percent of a manager's and her subordinates' time is spent negotiating with other subunits, while only 20 percent of their time is spent on tasks that are strictly within the jurisdiction of their work group.

Top management usually responds to such structural problems by creating new management positions in order to coordinate the many tasks that flow between subunits. In time, an extensive management hierarchy evolves. In fact, it resembles a light bulb more than a pyramid, as more and more high-level managers are assigned to coordinate more and more managers at the next level below them—who, in turn, have been assigned to coordinate the many managers below them, and so on. Only at the very bottom of the hierarchy has the *real* work of the organization been assigned to the workers. But these nonsupervisory members, because of the many tasks that flow between subunits, spend most of their time complaining that they cannot get their work done on time!

Properly aligning all three interfaces (strategic, structural, job), puts more control of the work in the hands of all organizational members. What previously seemed out of reach and therefore was experienced by members as *external* control can be transformed into *internal* control—by giving members direct access to the critical tasks that determine both job and organizational success. Recall that the first three tracks foster internal control—personal responsibility for success—through better management of the informal organization. Note that the last two tracks can foster additional internal control through better management of the *formal* organization—in this case, by directly controlling task flows.

At this point in the process, the participants in the strategy-structure track are struck by a revelation: Subunit boundaries are not cast in stone; they are cast in outdated assumptions about how to organize task flows. Now the participants are eager to consider alternative ways for designing subunits. In fact, they are anxious to begin devising alternative "initial" conclusions about structural configurations, whose underlying assumptions can be surfaced, classified, and synthesized. With assumptional analysis, a "final" design of subunits can be derived—one that will improve the alignment of strategy and structure throughout the organization.

One way to create alternative operational structures is to make use of MAPS—multivariate analysis, participation, and structure (Kilmann, 1977). This approach takes advantage of computer technology in performing the most computationally complex aspects of designing subunits: (1) identifying all work flows for tens of objectives, hundreds of tasks, and thousands of people and (2) creating subunits to contain the sequential and reciprocal flows. (See Mackenzie, 1986, for another approach to designing operational structures.)

Briefly, the participants in the strategy-structure track must develop an objectives dictionary and a task dictionary. The objectives dictionary lists all the objectives (with definitions) that must be accomplished in order to realize the firm's strategic plan; the task dictionary lists all the tasks (with definitions) that must be performed in order to accomplish the firm's objectives. It may take the participants a few days or even a few weeks to finish their initial draft of these dictionaries. Then members throughout the current operational structure are given a chance to examine and modify the initial lists (and definitions). Eventually, the two dictionaries together comprise items that are well understood by all members (no jargon, no ambiguities) *and* operationalize the firm's new strategic direction in a comprehensive manner. An organization's two dictionaries typically consist of 10 to 50 objectives and 50 to 250 tasks. (Examples of objectives and tasks were presented earlier in this chapter.)

It would take too much space to detail how the two dictionaries are developed into questionnaires and the way in which all organizational members (or a representative sample) are asked to indicate (on a seven-point rating scale) their ability to accomplish each objective and their corresponding need to perform each task. Similarly, this is not the place to show how members' responses to the MAPS questionnaires are used to create different structural alternatives. The interested reader is referred to another work (Kilmann, 1977) for a complete discussion of the methodology. Figure 16, shown previously, portrays one output of the MAPS analysis—which would be supplemented with appendixes listing the subset of objectives, tasks, and people assigned to each subunit in the organization. MAPS can provide a range of structural alternatives, however, by varying the number of subunits at each level in the hierarchy and by varying the number of hierarchical levels in the organization. Similarly, MAPS can provide alternative matrix arrangements as well as mixed designs by location, function, product, service, and time.

The alternative MAPS structures are often dramatically different from the current operational structure. New subunits are created to resolve structural interface problems that could not be resolved previously—even with interteam building. Some R&D tasks, for example, might be combined with several market research tasks and with other tasks concerning new production methods in order to form a new subunit: New Product Research and Design. After the participants in the strategy-structure track have had a chance to examine this new arrangement, they realize how much time has been spent trying to coordinate new product introductions: R&D has been conducting research that is too scientific according to the rest of the organization; marketing has been preoccupied with short-term sales objectives; manufacturing has continued to resist any changes that slow down day-to-day production.

After several radically different structural alternatives have been outlined (the current structure, several alternative MAPS structures, and any other proposed solutions), the participants in the strategy-structure track proceed with assumptional analysis. Following the debate of all assumptions underlying each "initial" conclusion, a synthesis group (S-group) is formed by including two representatives from each C-group. Once the S-group has derived the "final" operational structure by resolving any remaining differences on assumptions, by collecting any new information, and by flushing out the necessary details of the chosen solution, the other participants in the strategy-structure track are given the opportunity to make minor adjustments—as assumptions warrant. Then a formal proposal is presented to top management. Just as in the case of the strategic plan, if senior executives would like to make changes in the solution proposed by the participants in the strategy-structure track, they must offer new assumptions backed by new information.

### Implementing Structure

The well-seasoned participants in the strategy-structure track realize the absurdity of trying to implement change by having top management announce that the new structure—on paper—will be in effect on a particular date. Rather, it is only when members' behavior is guided by the new strategic direction with the new organization of resources that the proposed structure will truly be operational. In fact, implementing a structural solution is a complex problem in its own right, since such a change involves a difficult adjustment for most organizational members. Disbanding old work groups and forming new ones dramatically alter the distribution of power, friendships, and traditions in the organization. Consequently, management must be sensitive to members' anxieties: "Will I get along with the new people in my subunit? Will I be able to learn the new skills needed to manage people with different backgrounds and personalities? Will I still be an important asset to the company?" Recognizing these feelings and providing opportunities to work them through will ensure a smooth transition.

Just as there are alternative problem definitions that—if not analyzed properly—will result in defining errors, alternative approaches for implementing structural change—if not analyzed properly—will lead to implementing errors. In particular, implementing solutions without considering human nature and corporate culture will limit the potential benefits of the new structure.

Now the participants in the strategy-structure track are asked to devise alternative plans for implementing the new structure. To ensure that some innovative approaches will be considered, the participants sort themselves into the four Jungian personality groups—NF, NT, ST, and SF—discussed in Chapter Four. The implementation plans that are outlined in these subgroups become four very different "initial" conclusions. Each proposed plan addresses fundamental questions: What is meant by implementation, how long does it take, how does one know when it is complete, and is it ever complete? In their four Jungian C-groups, the participants then surface and classify their assumptions in order to support their proposed plan. Following the debate of assumptions across all the C-groups, an S-group is formed to synthesize any remaining differences on assumptions.

As a result of all its deliberations, the S-group usually agrees to these synthesized assumptions: (1) Members regard the prospect of strategy-structure change as a threat to their self-esteem and identity. (2) Members need to know, in advance, exactly what to expect during the entire process of implementing the new structure. (3) Members are more likely to change if the new situation can be defined as an improved situation from *their* point of view. (4) Members will change if sufficient time, emotional support, and developmental activities are provided so that they *can* change.

Based on these synthesized assumptions, the S-group deduces a "final" implementation plan that usually includes the following characteristics. First, the transition from the old to the new structure should proceed gradually (several months to one year in most cases), so that members have time to adjust—mentally and emotionally— to the new structure. Thus there is a rhythm and pace of change that can be nudged but not rushed: Too much change too quickly results in resistance; too little change too slowly leads to resignation.

Second, during the transition, participants in the strategy-structure track should continue to assess members' experiences and feelings about the new operational structure. As a result of these assessments, information about the process of change can be provided regularly according to members' needs. What are other subunits experiencing? What progress is being made throughout the organization? Honest answers to these questions will help put the human side of the endeavor in a realistic perspective. If members are uninformed or misinformed, they will assume the worst.

Third, participation should be extensive during the entire process of structural change so that members have a chance to improve and accept the new operational structure. For example, each new subunit of members can meet regularly to develop their assigned objectives and tasks into formal charters. These meetings can take place in a collateral arrangement, since most of the members' time is still being spent in the current operational structure. Moreover, group members can be involved in designing new control, budgeting, and planning systems (or adapting current systems) to give them the operating and strategic information they need for effective problem management in their subunit. (Participants in the strategy-structure track can be involved in designing or adapting the centralized systems for the whole organization.) Furthermore, the members in each subunit can be given an opportunity to participate in the design of their jobs. Not surprisingly, the more each job is defined by the same criteria as the design of each subunit—that is, containment of a total piece of work so that internal control is augmented—the more each job will maximize the potential for high performance and morale. In order to realize this potential, each job should guide the person to spend the right amount of time on the right tasks according to the right objectives.

Fourth, developing the right kind of documentation for each subunit—both formal charters and job descriptions—should be guided by what will achieve success in each case. While there is not a one-to-one relationship between personalities and jobs, it is useful to match the cognitive strengths of the person with the job's information-taking and decision-making requirements (as discussed in Chapter Four). The STs, for example, prefer considerable detail in guidelines and procedures—which fits well with jobs in a stable environment (such as manufacturing or accounting). The SFs prefer considerable detail on how to make contact with people—which fits well with jobs that require extensive social networks (such as personnel or sales). The NTs prefer only general guidelines on what new approach is needed for success—which fits well with jobs that require innovation and creativity (such as R&D or market research). The NFs prefer only general guidelines on what social goals are essential to accomplish—which fits well with jobs entailing community or institutional missions (such as public relations or environmental scanning).

And fifth, the more each subunit has changed—in terms of different objectives, tasks, and people—the more certain aspects of the earlier tracks must be addressed again. For example, the members in each new subunit can be assembled for additional meetings to agree on the cultural norms for the new subunit, since each member may have developed a somewhat different culture in his previous work group. Moreover, special skills training (management *and* technical) can be arranged to prepare members for their new work situation. Even if each member has participated in the previous team-building track, the new composition of members usually requires additional discussion on group process in order to develop cohesion, trust, and openness in the new subunit. But in most cases, there is little need for more *inter*team building with the new operational structure. The new subunits were purposely *designed* to be autonomous—linked by pool, not sequential and reciprocal task flows—thus minimizing the amount and frequency of intergroup activity.

## The Bottom Line

Placing the operational structure behind the strategic plan aligns the organization's resources (efficiency) in the right direction (effectiveness), which helps to make organizational members happy (morale). As major changes in the organization's setting develop in the future, however, another restructuring will be necessary as different strategic choices are made. With the problem management organization in place, members will be able to manage each strategy-structure adjustment thoroughly and systematically. Now, however, the organization will use another PMO to address its next immediate problem: designing a well-functioning, performance-based reward system. Here we close the circle by motivating and rewarding members for efficient and effective performance.

# 7

## The Reward System Track:

## Motivating High Performance and Sustaining All Improvements

In most organizations, reward systems are designed, implemented, and administered in a top-down authoritarian manner. As a result, the acceptance level of reward systems is often low, and the design of the system often fails to take into account important information about the preferences and desires of those who fall under the system. Under certain conditions, participation in reward system decisions is an approach that will produce better understanding of the system, a better system, and a high commitment to implement it.

—Lawler, 1981, p. 26

Organizations offer people numerous rewards in exchange for the behavior they provide and the results they produce. These rewards can be sorted into two types: intrinsic and extrinsic. Intrinsic rewards are the positive feelings a person gets while performing his job. If the job is interesting, exciting, and challenging, for example, the person experiences pleasure just by doing what the job entails. Extrinsic rewards are given formally by the organization rather than occurring naturally in the work setting. Salary, bonuses, paid vacations, fringe benefits, office furnishings, awards, promotions—all come to members from the organization rather than the job itself.

151

If the prior tracks have been conducted properly, every member has an opportunity to experience intrinsic rewards: The culture track encourages the development of trustworthy and gratifying interpersonal relationships (both within and between work groups); the management skills track ensures that members will be treated with respect by their superiors and will have the skills to tackle the challenging problems all around them; the team-building track provides each member with a cohesive and disciplined work group free from the disruptive effects of troublemakers; the strategy-structure track designs objectives and tasks into autonomous subunits, so members can control and, therefore, *see* the results of their efforts. Apart from these intrinsic rewards, the formal reward system can now be designed to allocate extrinsic rewards in a way that promotes both high performance and morale. On completion of the reward system track, not only will the current members prefer to remain in the organization and excel on the job, but the organization will be more attractive to prospective employees. Thus a well-functioning, performance-based reward system promotes the full utilization of both current and future human resources.

This chapter shows how the problem management organization (PMO) can be used to establish the right performance-based reward system. Moreover, by formally rewarding behavior that fosters the new culture, the new skills, and cooperative team effort, the reward system sustains all improvements. In this way, the various benefits that originated from implementing the five tracks will last beyond the present crew of managers, members, and consultants. Ultimately, if all members—both present and future—believe that the behavior they provide and the results they produce can lead to important intrinsic and extrinsic rewards, they will spend the right amount of time on the right tasks according to the right objectives—exactly what is required for organizational success.

### Understanding a Performance-Based Reward System

Objectively measuring each member's performance—and then equitably distributing rewards to members based on these measures—represents a most complex problem. Thus another version of the PMO should be used for the reward system track in order to minimize all the errors of problem management, particularly defining and implementing errors. Once the strategy-structure track has redesigned the organization's operational structure, the collateral structure for the PMO can be formed to represent this new arrangement of personnel. Thus even if members are spending most of their time in their old work groups as the new design of subunits is being implemented, the new reward system must be guided by the most recent alignment of objectives, tasks, and people.

Again it is the shadow track (consisting of the executives and other members who are responsible for the whole improvement program) that selects twenty-five or so participants to work on the reward system problem—a different set of participants from those who are working on the strategy-structure problem. The same criteria, however, are used for selection: The participants should represent all areas and levels in the organization (in this case, according to the newly designed operational structure); they should exemplify the desired norms and the use of problem management skills; they should have clout.

Once the participants in the reward system track have been assembled for their first on-the-job work session, material is presented on such topics as motivation and need theories, intrinsic and extrinsic rewards, reliable and valid measures, performance reviews and counseling sessions, and legal issues in the design and administration of reward systems. Moreover, alternative reward systems are examined that combine some of the following distinctions: piece rate versus hourly rate; hourly rate versus salary; skill-based pay versus job-based pay; cash bonuses versus stock options; individual versus group versus company-wide bonuses; gain sharing versus profit sharing; and fixed versus flexible fringe benefits. In most cases, both external consultants and internal human resource specialists instill in the participants a working knowledge of the purpose, design, and functioning of reward systems. During this first work session, the participants also review the diagnostic results that were presented by the consultants at the early stages of the improvement program. After having been exposed to the latest thinking in the field, participants find new meaning in the reward system barriers to success that were identified during the interview process.

In subsequent work sessions, the participants in the reward system track meet with their counterparts in the strategy-structure track to discuss their progress to date. Their interaction continues throughout the implementation of the new operational structure and the new reward system. This ongoing exchange of information helps to align *all* the formal systems in the organization. At the same time, the participants in the reward system track are required to maintain extensive two-way communication with the rest of the membership—a process that fosters organization-wide understanding and commitment to all proposed solutions.

As a result of all these activities and discussions, the participants in the reward system track develop a keen appreciation of the conditions that are essential to a performance-based reward system. To these participants, it quickly becomes obvious why all the prior tracks must precede the reward system track. As shown in Figure 20, ultimately it is the quality of the interpersonal relationship between every superior and his or her subordinates that fosters the success of a reward system. Yet performance reviews and counseling sessions—the reward system in *practice*—cannot be conducted effectively unless the prior tracks have accomplished their objectives. To convey this key point, the following sections present an explanation—organized according to each of the prior four tracks—of what the participants must learn about designing and implementing a performance-based reward system.

### The Impact of Culture on Reward Systems

Without an adaptive culture that fosters trust, information sharing, and receptiveness to change, members have little reason to believe in the formally documented reward system or their superior's use of any such system. In a dysfunctional culture, members believe (perhaps rightly so) that rewards are based on favoritism and politics, not on performance. Worse yet, when caught in a deep culture rut, members often impose strong sanctions on anyone who dares to defy work group norms that discourage high levels of performance. How does completion of the culture track help in-

Figure 20. Understanding a Performance-Based Reward System.

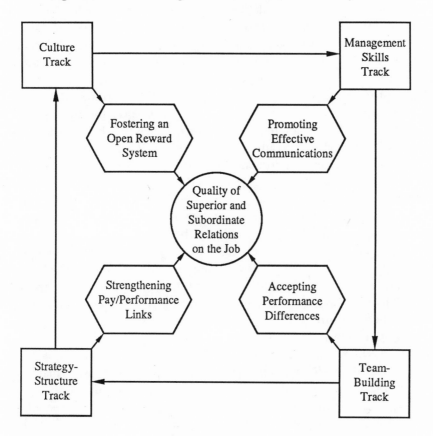

dividuals and work groups decide that it *is* worthwhile for them to work hard and do well? Consider the following.

Just as organizational performance is determined by all the categories in the Barriers to Success model (Figure 3, Chapter Two), individual performance is based on a similar set of factors: the person's motivation to work; whether the cultural norms of the work group support or restrict a person's motivation; the person's traits, skills, and ability to do his or her job; the amount of control the person has over the results of his work; and whether the person spends the right amount of time on the right tasks according to the right objectives.

It seems that a person's decision on how hard and how well to work derives from a deliberate thought process—at least until cultural forces take over. First she surveys the situation to see if there are any rewards available that suit her needs. If there are none, she either leaves the situation or does the minimum to remain as a member until she has a better alternative. If there *are* rewards that suit the person's needs, she then estimates the likelihood that she can do what it takes to receive them. In essence, the individual considers what the job requires, whether she has the ability to do the job, whether she can control the tasks that will lead to success, and how much time and effort she must invest to be successful. So long as she *believes* that the rewards will be forthcoming after she achieves a level of performance that she can control, the individual will expend all her effort and talent in the right direction—as outlined by her job and guided by her boss.

Where do such beliefs come from? The formation of beliefs about a reward system is affected more by cultural forces than by a simple cost-benefit analysis conducted by each individual member. If members do not receive the rewards they feel they deserve (based on their performance), the reward system loses some of its credibility. As members share these bad experiences with one another, they revise their collective beliefs—norms—about the reward system: Don't believe what top management says; around here, performance appraisal is *personal* appraisal. Even if the formal documents explicitly state that the distribution of rewards is based on performance, members usually rely on others' experiences and organizational stories when deciding who or what to believe. Consequently, there may be a big difference—a reward system gap— between what is written on paper and what the membership believes to be the current practice. How can this gap be closed? There must be trustworthy information. If information is not provided, people will invent it. This becomes a dangerous situation: The more that people are kept in the dark, the more that groups have the power to develop a social reality that is even more distorted than individual misconceptions.

Does the current reward system give members the information they need to judge its credibility? The participants in the reward system track are often startled when they realize that information about their pay system is held in complete secrecy—supported by cultural norms—and that most within-company comparisons regarding compensation are considered private matters. Although the participants realize that many people view wages and salaries as personal and confidential, they also recognize that there is a lot of room for variation between complete secrecy and full disclosure. Even if individual salaries are kept secret, most members would like to know the salary ranges of different job positions, the ranges of various bonuses, and the average percentages of salary increases. Moreover, it may be useful to make available—every year—the performance ratings of each individual in similar job classifications, along with the actual amount of his increase in salary and bonus, or just the percentage change in both. Such explicit information is absolutely critical for judging whether rewards indeed are based on performance. It is seldom necessary to show each person's actual salary, however, since that is determined by factors other than current performance: the amount and kind of education and training the person has received, the supply and demand conditions for the job at time of entry, and the previous levels of performance that have resulted in accumulated increases in base salary.

Porter, Lawler, and Hackman (1975, pp. 354-355) succinctly state the dilemma of secretive versus open compensation systems and suggest the probable impact of each approach on morale and, ultimately, performance:

> Secrecy about management pay rates seems to be an accepted practice in many organizations. However, organizations typically do not keep secret how other extrinsic rewards are administered. They do not keep promotions or who gets certain status symbols secret; in fact, they publicize these things. Why then do they keep salaries secret, and what are the effects of keeping them secret? It is usually argued that the pay of individuals is kept secret in order to increase pay satisfaction. Presumably secrecy increases satisfaction because if employees knew what other employees were earning, they would be more dissatisfied with their

own pay. This may in fact be true in organizations where the pay system is chaotic and cannot be rationally defended, but it is not clear that it is better to keep pay information secret when it is being well administered. In fact, there is evidence that keeping it secret may increase dissatisfaction and make it more difficult to use it as a motivator.

As a result of intense discussions on this controversial topic of open versus secretive reward systems, the participants realize how the culture track has already prepared the membership for a more open pay system. In fact, by the time the organization has progressed to the fifth track, most work groups have developed norms that encourage the open sharing of all information that pertains to complex business problems. Extending these norms to the public display of pay/performance information is not a difficult adjustment in most cases. Indeed, since the culture track has fostered open information and exchanges about everything else, it would seem rather hypocritical to keep members in the dark while they decide whether to risk their efforts for the promise of future rewards. Furthermore, participants often discover an added benefit that derives from establishing an open reward system: It helps keep everyone honest. When information is made available about the results of performance reviews and the distribution of extrinsic rewards, gross inequities or questionable practices become quite transparent. Thus superiors are more likely to administer an open reward system in an equitable manner, which further promotes trust between superiors and their subordinates.

### The Impact of Skills on Reward Systems

Without interpersonal skills, managers cannot conduct face-to-face performance reviews effectively. Defensiveness-producing styles of communication prevent subordinates from hearing the performance message. For similar reasons, managers cannot conduct effective counseling sessions to help subordinates improve their performance. Thus a well-functioning reward system requires that all managers are skilled at both communication and listening so they can motivate their subordinates to excel.

During the early stages of the management skills track (if suggested by the results of the diagnostic interviews), some of the classroom sessions introduced concepts and exercises for teaching managers how to give feedback to subordinates. Managers learned that feedback should be (1) asked for, (2) specific, (3) descriptive, (4) sincere, and (5) balanced. If the person receiving the comments explicitly initiated the request, he is likely to be in a receptive state of mind. Feedback that describes *specific* behavior tells the recipient exactly what is causing the problem without judging his worth. If the manager is sincere, the recipient will not be distracted by the suspicion of ulterior motives. And if the individual is told about behavior that should be encouraged—as well as behavior that should be discouraged—the discussion will be balanced and he will have one less reason to become defensive.

Participants in the reward system track usually agree that most feedback about performance is handled quite differently in *their* organization. Indeed, most performance appraisals are (1) not asked for, (2) general, (3) evaluative, (4) impersonal, and (5) one-sided. The subordinate's performance is reviewed when the organization or his boss decides it is time for an assessment—regardless of the subordinate's personal wishes or workload. The appraisal is very general. Perhaps it focuses on a summary score rather than detailing how the score was derived. The appraisal also seems highly evaluative, since the information is added to the employee's file without much discussion. Since the traditional appraisal comes top-down from superior to subordinate, reward decisions tend to be impersonal and thus can arouse defensiveness. And since the appraisal often concentrates on negative performance and overlooks the positives—as in "management by exception"—subordinates often feel that their performance is never quite good enough. Overcoming this negative feeling usually distracts employees from focusing on how to improve the results of their next review.

Even more problematic than ineffective feedback, however, is the manager who complains that she does not have enough time to conduct performance reviews and certainly does not have enough time to hold frequent counseling sessions with each subordinate. She has "more important" things to do. This cavalier approach to performance appraisal assumes that members know—completely and accurately—all their recent contributions and how to accomplish their objectives in the future. (Remember the simple machine view of the world?) Now, with a holographic view, managers recognize that all their employees need a constant stream of support, encouragement, and guidance in order to achieve job and organizational success.

The management skills track not only teaches managers how to give effective feedback but, in some cases, provides numerous role-playing exercises to develop skills specifically for discussing performance with subordinates. Through such practice sessions in a safe environment, managers become skilled in telling people, face to face, what went wrong and what went right.

### The Impact of Teams on Reward Systems

Without effective *teams*, superiors and subordinates are reluctant to engage in open group discussions on the results of performance reviews and the distribution of rewards—even if the pay/performance information is documented and made available to all group members. Furthermore, without the team-building track, each work group will *discourage* the boss from distributing different extrinsic rewards to its members according to their different performance ratings.

During the team-building track, the new culture and the new skills that were developed in classroom sessions—in peer groups— are transferred into the daily life of every work group. Each team has learned that all pertinent differences must be brought out in the open—with both superiors and subordinates present—in order to manage complex problems. Now the same approach must be used for addressing team members' different contributions to their individual and subunit objectives. Suppressing differences in their contributions not only prevents the low performers from getting the help they need; it also prevents the high performers from receiving the rewards they deserve.

Participants in the reward system track often realize that the high performers probably feel some resentment toward the organization, since their contributions do not result in more rewards than others receive. In fact, the high performers may have become the most dissatisfied workers while the low performers are the most satisfied. As a result, the high performers gradually leave the organization—since they usually have job alternatives—and the low performers remain behind. Certainly, such a migration of personnel neither represents a desirable outcome of human resources planning nor supports long-term organizational success.

Once the team-building track has achieved its purposes (controlling troublemakers and improving problem management efforts both within and between work groups), most group members appreciate the importance of openly discussing their performance differences with one another and sincerely helping each other to improve. The participants in the reward system track, however, usually see the fundamental paradox of differentiating each member's contributions while, at the same time, attempting to instill a team spirit. Perhaps the group's synergy will deteriorate if members are rewarded differently; perhaps members will be reluctant to draw attention to their individual accomplishments if the team approach is emphasized continually. In general, nonetheless, most work groups do accept the importance of maintaining a healthy tension between these two opposing forces—thus providing the organization with the best of both worlds: high-performance *teams* that can manage complex problems with an open acknowledgment of all kinds of differences among *individuals*. The challenge is to design a reward system that keeps the team/individual paradox alive and well without favoring either side.

## The Impact of Strategy-Structure on Reward Systems

Participants in the reward system track arrive at the obvious conclusion that pay and other extrinsic rewards cannot be linked to performance if performance cannot be measured objectively. An objective measure—in the form of a numerical score—consists of two essential qualities: reliability and validity. Reliability concerns whether the same number is obtained by independent raters. Validity concerns whether the number captures the true and complete value of the subunit's (or team's or individual's) contribution to organizational success.

*Every* subunit in the organization produces something that can be measured reliably. Finance completes a certain number of reports every year; advertising places a certain number of ads; R&D obtains a certain number of patents; manufacturing produces a certain number of units; marketing sells a certain number of products. But the key question is: Are these reliable numbers reflecting the right thing to measure? Only if a numerical score captures the whole domain of each subunit's expected behavior and results—its assigned set of tasks and objectives—and shows a clear link between the numerical score and an objective measure of organizational success (via each stakeholder's criteria as operationalized in the strategic plan) is the reliable measure also valid and, hence, objective.

Often, certain measures are selected to assess each subunit's performance due to their reliability, not necessarily because they measure the right things. Thus the ease in finding a reliable measure often overshadows the difficulty of establishing a valid one—which suggests that many performance measures may be rooted in a false assumption: If it can be measured easily, it must be right.

Participants in the reward system track, drawing from their understanding of objective measures and their continuing dialogue with participants in the strategy-structure track, now experience a fundamental insight: When there are significant task flows between all subunits, it is virtually impossible to establish an objective measure of performance—one that is both reliable and valid—other than for the whole organization. Consider the case in which an organization's subunits are designed according to functional specialties. Every subunit is so interrelated with other subunits that performance cannot be assessed for any single subunit; each subunit's true value to the organization is completely intermingled with its task flows to and from other subunits. Consequently, each subunit's output may be of value only when it is interconnected—sequentially and reciprocally—with the outputs of other subunits. An R&D unit, for example, has little value unless its outputs are developed into commercial products by engineering, which next are produced by manufacturing, and which then are sold and distributed to customers by sales. When several interrelated subunits are formed into a more encompassing unit, it is much easier to construct objective measures—such as organizing all the business functions into one product line that becomes a separate profit center.

Lawler (1981, p. 86) offers a useful guideline that combines smaller subunits into larger "performance" units—by taking into account the nature of task flows between subunits—so that objective measures of performance are possible:

> One way to identify performance units is to start with individuals at the bottom of the organization and work up through the hierarchy until a level is reached at which (1) performance is clearly measurable in relatively objective terms, (2) no important interdependencies which affect that individual's work fall into parallel parts of the organization, and (3) the individual controls most of the factors that influence his or her performance results. At this point, a performance-based pay system should be considered— be it at the individual, group, or even divisional level.

A special problem is created, however, when performance is measured close to the organizational level: The link between performance and rewards becomes more and more remote in the eyes and minds of the members. In essence, if objective measures of performance are far removed from the daily work that each person can control within his own subunit, a member will have great difficulty seeing how his own effort—as one of a thousand others who are formed into one large performance unit—directly contributes to such objective measures as earnings per share or return on investment at the corporate level.

Now participants in the reward system track appreciate how the successful completion of the strategy-structure track sets the stage for the objective measurement of performance as close to the individual level as possible—given the nature and extent of task flows. The more the organization is structured to contain the troublesome task flows *within* subunits, the more that objective performance measures can be constructed for these smaller—autonomous—subunits. With minimal task flows between subunits, the discrete outputs of each unit can easily be added together—pooled—at some later time. Moreover, the more each job has been designed to contain a complete piece of work under the direct control of the jobholder, the more performance can be measured objectively at the individual level.

Participants in the reward system track must accept, however, that objective measures of *short-term* performance (one year or less) cannot capture all the contributions required of members for *long-term* organizational success (several years or more)—no matter how perfectly the organization is structured into autonomous subunits. The best predictor of high performance in the future may not be short-term results—because what satisfies stakeholders this year may not satisfy them next year (due to dynamic complexity). Instead, the best predictor is whether members are behaving in all the ways that can be expected to resolve any complex problem—business, technical, or organizational—that might materialize in the future. This behavior, highlighted throughout the improvement program, can be measured objectively—via various rating forms—if special attention is given to reliability and validity. Peers in each work group, for example, can assess how well each member contributes to (1) supporting an adaptive culture, (2) improving her skills for people management and problem management, (3) adding to the team spirit of his work group and that of the whole organization, and (4) facilitating the flow of tasks and information for any remaining sequential and reciprocal links between her subunit and other units in the organization. Thus, by combining a measure of short-term results with a measure of all the behavior that has an impact on long-term organizational success, one overall—holistic—measure of a member's performance is now possible.

### Establishing a Performance-Based Reward System

Once the participants in the reward system track fully appreciate all the foregoing material (as well as the possibilities and legalities of different reward systems), they generally agree that a large organization with several divisions in different markets will not be best served by one centralized reward system. While there should be some shared policies and procedures across all subunits—in order to achieve some form of equity and to aid in human resources planning—each subunit may need to have a somewhat different system to match its uniqueness (its setting, objectives, tasks, culture, personalities). Nevertheless, a creative synthesis between a corporate reward policy and subunit-by-subunit reward systems can be established for the organization.

If any members of the organization are unionized, a special effort can be made to remove the constraints imposed by collective bargaining agreements. If this is not feasible, then some parts of the organization will be governed by union contracts (even if these represent a non-performance-based reward system) while others will be free to consider alternative performance-based reward systems. But the mere existence of union membership should not preclude the possibility of gaining union/management cooperation—which is becoming the rule rather than the exception in today's global, competitive marketplace.

## Designing the Reward System

Now the participants in the reward system track are asked to devise alternative reward systems for their organization—in the form of general concepts or frameworks, not the detailed reward systems that will be developed by each subunit. To ensure that a wide range of approaches will be considered, the participants may subdivide into the four Jungian personality groups—NF, NT, ST, and SF—discussed earlier. The general reward systems that are proposed by these subgroups become four very different "initial" conclusions. Every proposal addresses fundamental questions: What is motivation, what is performance, what is measurement, what is a reward, and how does the organization motivate high performance—measured objectively—with its extrinsic and intrinsic rewards? In their four Jungian conclusion groups (C-groups), the participants then surface and classify their assumptions in order to support their proposed reward systems. Following the debate of assumptions across all C-groups, a synthesis group (S-group) resolves any remaining differences on assumptions.

As a result of all its deliberations, the S-group usually agrees to these synthesized assumptions:

1.  In some ways, people are the same; in other ways, people are different.

2.  People are the same in that their self-worth is based on both internal criteria (identity, self-confidence, stable self-perceptions, and ways of looking at life) *and* external criteria (university degrees, job positions, titles, career success, houses, cars, and financial net worth).

3.  People are the same in that their work life can be a primary means of satisfying their external criteria for self-worth and can be an important forum for self-expression as well—if their work environment provides the extrinsic and intrinsic rewards they value. Otherwise, people will do the minimum to remain in the organization and will satisfy their needs in other settings.

4.  People are different with regard to the extent of their total self-worth (combining both internal and external criteria) and, as a result, they respond quite differently to performance reviews and counseling sessions with their superiors.

5.  People are different with regard to their need for various extrinsic rewards and the pleasure they experience from various intrinsic rewards.

6.  Most people cannot judge the value of extrinsic rewards without making numerous comparisons to other people in similar—and different—situations. Most people can judge the value of intrinsic rewards without making social comparisons—if they feel a high degree of self-worth. Otherwise, they also need to affirm their experiences with others.

7.  Most people want to own their efforts (the means of production) rather than rent themselves to the organization. People differ on what they are willing to risk in order to own rather than rent their efforts.

8.  Most people are reasonable in what they expect to receive from the organization—if they are treated respectfully, sincerely,

and honestly, and if they are given the opportunity to understand and influence the key decisions that affect them.

9.  Most people begin to take notice of a 5 percent change in bonus or salary, are pleased with a 10 percent change, and are affected deeply by a change greater than 25 percent. The same reactions apply when people become aware of the different percentages that the highest performers versus the lowest performers receive in bonuses and salary changes.

10. Most people greatly appreciate the "little things" in life—a smile, a thank you, a handshake, a pat on the back—so long as these gestures are genuine.

Based on these synthesized assumptions, the S-group deduces a "final" reward system that usually includes the following characteristics. First, the whole organization will be guided by a unified corporate reward policy of measuring performance and distributing rewards to people based on performance. Typically, this policy encourages a more open reward system than previously was the case, so members are given the information and comparisons that promote the credibility of the new reward system. The policy also expresses a strong commitment to do whatever it takes to keep the link between rewards and performance absolutely clear in everyone's mind. Moreover, the policy requires that each member's performance rating includes an assessment of both short-term and long-term contributions (results and behavior, respectively) and uses multiple inputs to derive such measures whenever it is possible to do so (from peers, superiors, subordinates, customers, clients). Furthermore, the policy requires that every manager's performance rating includes an assessment of how well he conducts performance reviews and counseling sessions with his subordinates. (Such an assessment can be provided—anonymously, perhaps—by the subordinates to their boss's own superior.)

Second, within this broad framework of corporate reward policy, every autonomous subunit in the organization—wholly owned subsidiaries, lines of business, business units, product lines, profit centers—has the freedom to design a special reward system according to what will lead to success in each case. Just as each new subunit is encouraged to develop its formal charter, job designs, and desired norms (see Chapter Six), a participative process is now applied to design a custom-tailored, performance-based reward system. The participants in the reward system track will facilitate this process, subunit by subunit, so that the whole membership is guided by the same knowledge of reward systems that the participants themselves have acquired. Naturally, human resource experts from either inside or outside the company can be used to ensure that all technical guidelines are followed and all legal requirements are met.

Third, while different combinations of reward packages are designed for different subunits, many share similar aspects. The formula that determines a person's overall performance rating might look rather complex on the surface. But close inspection would reveal that it tries to capture the true and complete value of the person's short-term and long-term contributions. The formula might include individual, group, departmental, divisional, and organizational assessments of results, for example—with more weight given to the results that are closest to the jobholder. The formula might also include quarterly, annual, and five-year assessments of behavioral contributions—with more weight given to those behaviors that predict future performance. Management by objectives (MBO) might be used to operationalize the results aspects of the formula, while behaviorally anchored rating scales (BARS) could be used to pinpoint the behavioral aspects of the formula (Gibson, Ivancevich, and Donnelly, 1988). All specialized reward systems must include the specific procedures that will be used to validate and adjust the formula periodically as the subunit's setting, objectives, tasks, and culture change.

Fourth, in order for members to make well-informed decisions on how they can achieve high scores on their formula, they must have access to relevant business information (financial, marketing, manufacturing, human resource, and the like)—supported by proper training and specific guidelines for using this information in a responsible way. Thus the formal reward system—supported by control systems, budgeting systems, planning systems, and information systems—plays an integral role in a holographic approach to on-the-job problem management.

And fifth, each subunit offers a wide variety of extrinsic and intrinsic rewards to satisfy different people's needs and personalities. Typically a cafeteria-style benefit package is offered to members so they can adjust their health insurance, life insurance, pension plans, and other fringe benefits according to their changing needs. Moreover, various educational and career development programs are included in the total package of rewards provided to organizational members. When consistent with the demands of the job, flexible working hours and work-at-home privileges are additional options that might be made available. In some cases, skill-based pay is provided both to reward those who acquire additional expertise and to develop a multiskilled work force that can adjust quickly to changing circumstances. In other cases, an all-salaried work force is established in order to treat employees as self-reliant professionals. In a few cases, employees are offered stock options so they can invest in their own efforts in their own organization.

The range of cash bonuses distributed to members can vary tremendously, depending on the performance formula and the success of both individual and team efforts. Annual bonuses are often a convincing incentive in a performance-based reward system, since they can easily range from 0 to 100 percent of salary. Spot bonuses, given for a short burst of effort or a special accomplishment, are excellent reinforcements to the pay-for-performance link. Salary changes, incidentally, while desirable for the sake of security, are less effective for motivating outstanding performance, since increases in salary for one year continue into the future—and rarely do organizations withhold salaries as they withhold bonuses. Finally, all members are encouraged to afford one another the simple pleasures in life: warmth, caring, thoughtfulness, appreciation, and kindness.

### Implementing the Reward System

While the new reward system for each autonomous subunit might look very good on paper, the issue—as always—is whether behavior in the organization is guided by the documented system. Implementation—translating paper into behavior—is a complex problem, especially for a system that is designed to motivate and reward high performance. The various plans for implementing the new reward system, therefore, should be developed with the use of assumptional analysis. Not surprisingly, the "final" conclusion for implementing the new reward system is usually similar to the one derived for implementing the new operational structure, as discussed in the previous chapter: The process takes time (perhaps several months to a year), and members' feelings about the process should be monitored regularly. Further, extensive participation should be encouraged so that improvements in the new system are developed and accepted by the members. Personality differences should be taken into account throughout the implementation process. And, naturally, portions of the earlier tracks should be conducted again if further refinement of a subunit is deemed necessary.

The key issue to consider in implementing the new reward system, as shown in Figure 20, is the quality of each superior/ subordinate relationship—especially when the superior officially presents the results of the performance appraisal to his subordinate and then counsels him on what to do differently during the next work cycle. To maintain a quality interaction between these two unequal partners, one must learn to distinguish the evaluative component (when performance ratings, bonuses, and salary changes are communicated) from the learning component (when feedback is given on how behavior and results can be improved). While these two components usually are discussed together in the same meeting, they really need to be handled in separate meetings and to be separated in time as well. It seems that a subordinate being reviewed by a superior raises sensitive questions and underlying anxieties about one's self-worth—especially since our society labels people according to the work they do:

> Performance appraisal systems are often used to accomplish two conflicting objectives: determining the rewards an individual will receive and providing counseling and feedback for purposes of improvement and development. These goals call for different discussion emphases and can have different effects on the employee. When the performance evaluation is used in determining the rewards an individual will

receive, employees have a reason for defending their performance and presenting themselves in the best possible light. Under such circumstances, they are likely to give invalid data about themselves in order to look good. As such, the performance appraisal serves neither purpose well [Allenbaugh, 1983, pp. 22-23].

The participants in the reward system track usually recommend that each subunit manager meet with his or her work group to discuss how the two types of meeting can be designed and scheduled to meet the organization's requirements and the needs of its members. What will be expected in both meetings should be spelled out in advance so everyone will know how to prepare for them—mentally and emotionally.

Regarding performance reviews, these meetings should be scheduled according to the rhythm and flow of work in each subunit. While it is often convenient for an organization to establish one review each year, this plan may not be desirable if divisions, departments, and work groups have different types of jobs with different completion cycles. In a dynamic work setting, it might be useful to review performance more frequently. If several performance cycles take place in a year, holding only annual reviews means that opportunities are missed to adjust performance from one cycle to the next. Instead, a subunit might establish these agreements: The manager will meet with each member once a month to review performance results, while the full performance review will take place every six months; any member, upon request, can see her file; any member can request an appeals process, without any negative consequences, if she disagrees with the results of her full performance review.

Regarding counseling sessions, the superior and subordinates in each subunit usually agree to frequent face-to-face discussions to clarify expectations, suggest improvements, and give encouragement. These discussions focus on culture, assumptions, skills, styles, behavior, attitudes, and teamwork. Often these barriers to success have been identified during the previous performance review. The idea is to provide a constant stream of emotional support and effective feedback so that members can improve their performance—in terms of both efficiency (the proper allocation of time on tasks) and effectiveness (completing the right tasks according to the right objectives). A subunit, therefore, might establish these agreements: Each member can arrange a counseling session with his boss whenever he needs more feedback and discussion. If the manager thinks a subordinate needs help, he should suggest that they sit down and discuss "how things are going." But it is up to the member to decide when this meeting should take place.

Above all, it is essential to establish how initial understandings can be adjusted as the situation changes. In a holographic world, new events mean that jobs and formulas must be modified. It would be unfair to hold a member accountable for an objective that is outdated or irrelevant. Instead, there should be a procedure that allows for negotiation and change—not as an excuse for failing to attain a realistic objective but as an acknowledgment of a fast-paced environment.

### The Bottom Line

As a result of completing the reward system track, members receive extrinsic rewards for performing well in their new organization in a new way according to a new culture. Coupled with the intrinsic rewards they experience automatically since the earlier tracks have been implemented, a salient reward package is available to everyone. Moreover, every superior and subordinate will have developed a vastly improved relationship in which trust and candor enable not only performance problems to be aired, but all other organizational problems as well. Perhaps the last time this experience occurred, if only for a moment, was when the members first opened their minds and hearts to an external consultant during the face-to-face diagnostic interviews at the early stages of the improvement program. Now, five tracks later, the consultant is bypassed. He is no longer needed. In fact, the new superior/subordinate relationship works much better for ongoing problem management than does a brief interview with a stranger. The improvement effort has been internalized, and it will last with continuing cycles of planned change. This is what adapting to dynamic complexity is all about.

# 8

## Managing the
## Completely Integrated Program:
### The Successful Experience
### at Eastman Kodak

Kodak's definition of market intelligence encompasses
functions that go well beyond traditional market research. Of
course, we have to give decision-makers the data they need to
more accurately define problems and assess early market
signals. But we are also accountable for developing the process
by which Kodak identifies and defines market information
needs. The goal, as expressed by top management, is to enable
Kodak "to sail ahead of the wind in an increasingly competitive market." We help managers become "proactive" rather
than "reactive." We try to dig out the assumptions behind our
market planning and to reduce the uncertainties.
—Barabba, 1984, p. 11

The previous five chapters have presented the theories and methods
that make up the five tracks, one chapter at a time. Now we must
return to the holographic aspects of the complete program—to put
all the interrelated pieces back together again. Managing beyond
the quick fix requires an integrated understanding of individual,
group, and organizational dynamics—an understanding that can be
fully appreciated only with a live example. This concluding chapter
presents the story of the Eastman Kodak Company, where the five
tracks were implemented for the corporate function of market
intelligence. Just as the completely integrated program is organized

into the five stages of planned change (Chapter Two), the application at Kodak is presented as (1) initiating the program, (2) diagnosing the problems, (3) scheduling the tracks, (4) implementing the tracks, and (5) evaluating the results.

## Background

In 1880, Kodak's first product—Eastman Dry Plates—was introduced into the marketplace. In 1888, Kodak's first camera—Number One Kodak—followed suit. Then, in 1900, Kodak created a mass market for photography with its soon-to-be-famous Brownie camera. For the next eighty years, Kodak dominated the market for cameras, film, and photographic paper by efficiently using a centralized, functionally designed organization that is perfectly suited to a predictable world. Then, circa 1980, the world changed: Dynamic complexity—fostered by worldwide accessibility, worldwide interconnectedness, and foreign competition—threatened both the viability of Kodak's long-standing structure and the appropriateness of its self-contained culture (Chakravarty and Simon, 1984). Electronic imaging, in particular, became a real alternative to silver halide photography. Then along came Fuji—a major Japanese player and fierce competitor in Kodak's key photographic markets.

On July 1, 1983, Colby H. Chandler succeeded Walter A. Fallon as chairman of the board and chief executive officer of Eastman Kodak. On November 16, 1984, Kodak announced a new strategic focus accompanied by a new operational structure of subunits that would go into effect on January 1, 1985. In the words of Chairman Chandler and President Kay R. Whitmore: "We intend to be a world-class competitor in the markets we serve. We are driving to become the world's premier imaging and information systems company. We are confident our new organization will help us meet those goals, and that the energy and spirit of Kodak people will make this new organization work" ("Photo Division Reorganized . . . ," 1984, p. 8). The reorganization of the photographic division affected 80 percent of the company—the other 20 percent comprised the chemical division.

The new Photographic and Information Management Division—in sharp contrast to Kodak's old organization by function—is organized into three large business groups: Photographic Products Group, Commercial and Information Systems Group, and Diversified Technologies Group. Each business group consists of several lines of business (LOBs)—with profit and loss responsibility—that are related through shared technology, market emphasis, or strategic approach. The three business groups are supplemented by two new operational units: Worldwide Manufacturing and Support Operations, and Customer and Marketing Support Operations ("Kodak Reorganizes . . . ," 1984). Reporting to Customer and Marketing Support Operations is Market Intelligence (MI). This support function—consisting of some 125 information specialists—provides information services to the entire organization and serves as the clearinghouse for all database activity in the new division.

### Initiating the Program

In September 1984, just a few months before the reorganization of Kodak was announced to the public, I was contacted by Vince Barabba, the director of Market Intelligence. Barabba had made use of my theories and methods for organization design and development in the 1970s when he was director of the U.S. Bureau of the Census during the Nixon administration and again during the Carter administration. Following the completion of the 1980 census, Barabba joined Kodak for the explicit purpose of developing the new corporate function of market intelligence. After he read *Beyond the Quick Fix* (Kilmann, 1984a) in August 1984, he thought that such an integrated program could be beneficial to the rapidly growing MI—first, by revealing what organizational barriers to success might be preventing MI from contributing fully to Kodak's new organization and, second, by removing any barriers via a specially designed application of the five tracks.

Although Barabba was well acquainted with the philosophy and requirements of my approach, other key managers were not. Consequently, he scheduled a half-day guest lecture for me at the end of September at Kodak's corporate headquarters in Rochester, New York. In this session, he asked me to present my holographic framework to several executives in marketing and a few directors in

market intelligence. Since Kodak's way of talking about organizational success uses the language of organization-wide quality
(whereas other companies use the language of productivity,
innovation, performance, excellence, or competitiveness), I
presented my approach in this context: how the organizational
barriers to success (Figure 3) can stand in the way of assessing
consumer needs, designing products that satisfy these needs,
manufacturing products that conform to the designers' exact
specifications with minimal defects or rejects, and then selling and
distributing the right products to the right customer in the right
quantity at the right time. In general, I thought the people in the
audience were receptive to my presentation; they seemed to grasp
why quality improvement in an organization requires (1) a holistic
framework to understand the essence of organizational life and (2)
an integrated program to manage that essence for long-term
organizational success.

In November 1984, just after Kodak's new strategy and
structure were announced, I was invited back to corporate headquarters in order to make a similar presentation to MI directors and
other executives who could not attend the September meeting. By
mobilizing the support of the key people who understood the
central role that MI would play in the new organization, Barabba
was laying the foundation for initiating the program in MI.

During this meeting I learned that, as of January 1, 1985, MI
would be organized into the same three areas as the three business
groups of the company: MI for Photographic Products, MI for
Commercial and Information Systems, and MI for Diversified
Technologies. These three groups in MI would also be subdivided
into smaller units to parallel the respective LOBs. As shown in
Figure 21, the organization of MI would mirror the organization of
Kodak. In particular, most members in MI would report both to an
MI director and to a Kodak manager—for each LOB in each
business group. Besides this mirrored matrix, MI also would
contain a core group, referred to as divisional market intelligence,
which would be an information service for corporate management
and a shared resource for all three business groups in MI.

Shortly after this November meeting, the twelve directors in
MI agreed that the diagnostic stage of planned change should be

Figure 21. The Organization of Market Intelligence (MI)
at Eastman Kodak: A Mirrored Matrix.

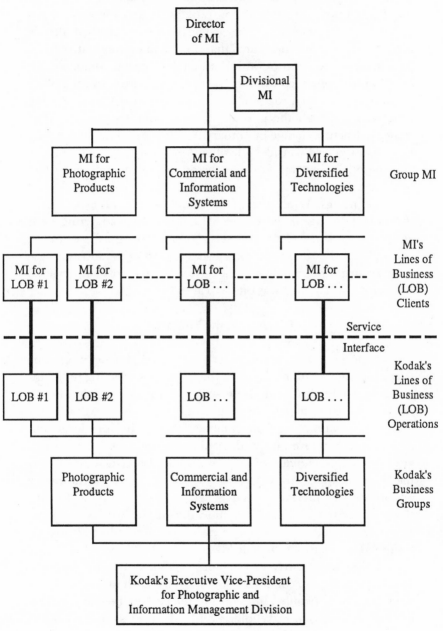

conducted in December and that the results should be presented in January 1985. In a phone conversation with Barabba, I admitted that I was a little surprised at how rapidly the decision process was proceeding. He assured me that extensive discussions had already taken place on the topic and that Phil Samper, executive vice-president of the Photographic and Information Management Division (the new organization), was very supportive of MI's plans to proceed with the program. I then questioned the timing of the program—given all the uncertainties surrounding the scheduled strategy-structure change in January. Barabba noted that the timing issue had received considerable attention as well. In fact, both he and the other directors felt that the advent of major change had made everyone in MI more receptive to introspection and new ways of doing things. While the LOBs would be struggling to define themselves during the next year, MI too would be analyzing itself and shaping its new identity. Besides, as Barabba argued, I would be able to learn about all the critical issues that affect the success of the improvement program during the upcoming diagnostic interviews. It seemed that Barabba was one step ahead of me.

### Diagnosing the Problems

The interview schedule was developed during numerous telephone conversations in which the criteria for selecting individuals were established and choices were made. It was decided to interview approximately 50 of the 125 members in MI—all MI directors and numerous representatives from all the other levels and areas in MI. Moreover, it was decided to interview some twenty-five key external stakeholders of the new organization (such as Samper, the three business group vice-presidents, and most of the newly appointed vice-presidents and general managers of the LOBs). Based on the availability of personnel during the first two weeks in December, a total of sixty-four interviews were scheduled (forty-six inside MI and eighteen outside MI).

I conducted thirty-six one-hour interviews and my associate, Teresa Joyce Covin, conducted twenty-eight. Each of us spoke to a cross section of people although my interview schedule included more of the external stakeholders while Teresa's sample included more of the internal ones. After we conducted all the interviews, we prepared separate diagnostic reports from our extensive notes. Then we met to discuss our similarities and differences in diagnostic findings so that we could synthesize what we had learned into one holographic view of MI's channels and barriers to success.

In January 1985, I presented the diagnostic results first to Barabba and later to the other directors in MI. I began by noting the channels to success (those positive qualities of the organization that would be the foundation for learning and change throughout the entire improvement effort): MI members expressed a strong loyalty to the company and felt a basic conviction that the company will succeed in whatever it does. MI members felt that they worked in a challenging environment and, perhaps because MI was still so new, they were quite optimistic about the possibilities for change and improvement. Moreover, MI members believed that their unit had strong top-management support. Unanimously, MI members acknowledged the critical role Barabba was playing in the success of the market intelligence function through his charismatic leadership. Of special significance to the improvement program, MI members viewed my appearance on the scene as just one more innovative example of Barabba's desire to do the best for Kodak and the MI organization.

The rest of my formal presentation concentrated on the various barriers to organizational success that had been identified during the diagnostic interviews. Since Kodak's new organization had been officially in place only since January 1, 1985 (and would not be fully operational until some time later), the interviews revealed numerous uncertainties concerning the impact that such a fundamental change would have on MI—both short term and long term. Consequently, many of the barriers to success were *anticipated* (listed as questions) rather than *actual* (listed as statements).

Regarding the setting, I highlighted two critical questions that were asked by virtually everyone we interviewed: Does MI really understand the needs of the customer? Does MI really understand the needs of its LOB clients? The implicit answer to these questions suggested that MI must improve (1) its understanding of the worldwide marketplace and (2) the quality of information it provides to LOB decision makers. Otherwise, MI's impact on Kodak's decision making would be limited.

Regarding the strategic barriers to success, the diagnostic interviews posed questions that revealed significant uncertainties surrounding the reorganization and what it meant for MI: Does MI have a clear understanding of its own strategic mission in helping the LOBs achieve their business objectives? Regarding a specific market research question, for example, should MI provide only the data analysis, make a specific recommendation, or make the decision itself? Will MI's strategy be translated into a well-documented set of plans and priorities that will guide all major decision making in MI—such as the allocation of resources to long-term studies or whether to accept contracts for certain short-term projects? Should MI's strategy be expanded to encompass business intelligence or business research? Essentially, it seemed that MI's strategic mission was not well understood by most members below the director level.

Regarding the structural barriers to success, the diagnostic interviews revealed additional uncertainties: How will the three levels in the MI hierarchy (see Figure 21) affect the speed and quality of decision making and action taking? Will all the essential communication links across the areas and levels in MI be defined, documented, and used effectively? Presently, it appeared that MI members did not have the work procedures and job descriptions they needed to guide their daily efforts and make the best use of their time and talent. Furthermore, members wondered whether MI could outlive its current leader: It seemed that Barabba himself was the driving force behind MI's credibility at Kodak rather than the function—or the structure—itself.

Regarding the reward system barriers to success, the diagnostic interviews revealed that people in Kodak are paid for being a member of the organization, not for their contributions to performance objectives. It seemed that people who delivered consistently outstanding performance did not receive significantly more rewards than those who did not. Perhaps this *non*-performance-based reward system had not interfered with Kodak's success in the past, but the people we interviewed certainly realized that a *performance*-based system was mandatory for achieving success in a competitive world. Many people also worried that MI had not designed specific career paths offering its members different job experiences and learning opportunities.

Regarding the management skills barriers to success, the diagnostic interviews revealed a number of questions to be addressed during an improvement effort: Do members have the people management skills to encourage disagreement and debate and to manage their differences in a productive way? Do members have the skills to tackle complex problems and hidden assumptions when they define and address the changing information needs of their LOB clients? It seemed that most MI members, who had received their formal training in specialized technical areas, could benefit from additional skill development in people management and problem management. I sensed, for example, that skills had to be developed in these areas: communicating nondefensively, fostering candor, managing conflict, motivating others, planning work, setting priorities, and conducting meetings.

Regarding the cultural barriers to success, the diagnostic interviews revealed that Kodak's self-contained, technical orientation from the past must be transformed into a market-driven, business orientation for the future. Would MI members continue to see the world with American blinders, or would the culture enable members to see a worldwide marketplace and act accordingly? Would the culture encourage the open expression of conflict and disagreements, or would it continue to reinforce politeness? Furthermore, since the function of market intelligence had increased in size and scope so quickly in just a few years, many members did not know one another. In fact, MI's culture seemed to foster impersonal social relationships on the job, which hampered trust, cooperation, group spirit, and a sense of community. Another side-effect of this social distance between members was that MI's culture seemed to encourage the withholding of information among its subunits. Moreover, MI appeared to have two classes of citizens—Salary I personnel (clerical and technical) and Salary II personnel (managers and professional analysts)—which further restricted cooperative effort and information sharing. Lastly, there was tremendous cultural pressure on individuals and groups to be busy at all times—without considering whether all the hard work was contributing to performance according to a clearly understood strategic mission.

Regarding group barriers to decision making and action taking, several questions were raised during the diagnostic interviews that derived from all the preceding barriers to success: When should decisions be made by individuals and when should decisions be made by groups? Would the meetings include those who have the relevant information and expertise for the complex problems being addressed? Would meetings include those whose commitment is essential for implementing whatever decisions are made? It seemed that many meetings in MI did not motivate members to participate. The process for group decision making was described as unplanned, inefficient, wandering, and tough to manage without clear objectives and priorities.

After the directors had discussed all these diagnostic results, they realized—even more than before—just how critical the market intelligence function would be to the success of the new organization. While the directors were pleased that the interviews had affirmed the many channels to success that had made MI an attractive organization, numerous interconnected barriers to success were working against them in every category in the Barriers to Success model—both actual and anticipated. Consequently, Barabba and the directors decided to begin the improvement program as soon as possible. Although a few directors suggested delaying the program until the new LOBs had time to form, most of the directors thought that MI should be proactive in shaping its future.

### Scheduling the Tracks

The following week, in mid-January 1985, I was asked to prepare a detailed outline of how the five tracks would be scheduled to remove all the barriers to success. Figure 22 shows the scheduling of the five tracks applied to MI, including the shadow track.

All 125 members in MI were scheduled to participate in the first three tracks, but the natural work groups would be separated into Salary I and Salary II subgroups for the culture track and the skills track. The diagnostic interviews, as mentioned earlier, had

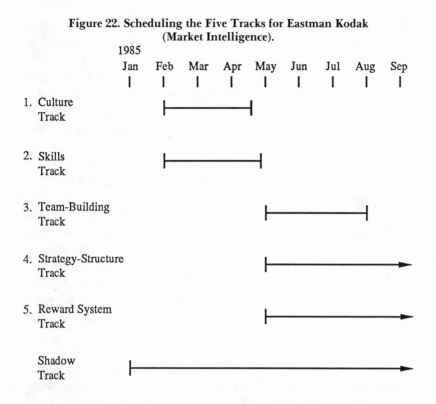

Figure 22. Scheduling the Five Tracks for Eastman Kodak (Market Intelligence).

revealed that there were two classes of citizens in MI. Indeed, Salary II persons (analytical and management types) were reluctant to acknowledge the talents and capabilities of Salary I persons (clerical and technical types). As a result, Salary I persons were less assertive in front of the more educated and higher-ranking members in the Salary II classification. After these status barriers to success were removed during the first two tracks (in a safe learning environment), the subgroups would be reunited in the team-building track (to apply what was learned in MI's natural work groups).

The culture track was scheduled for three workshops: one full day in February, March, and April 1985. (Each workshop would be conducted in three sessions of some 40 persons each in order to accommodate all 125 members of MI in an effective classroom arrangement; this format was continued for most of the first three tracks of the program.) The first culture workshop would enable each subgroup in MI to identify culture-gaps and develop a sanctioning system that would enforce the switch from actual to desired norms. The second workshop would assess the progress to date on developing a new culture and would enable each subgroup to revise, if necessary, its desired norms and its sanctioning system. The third workshop would involve another assessment of progress to date and provide additional steps to ensure that any remaining culture-gaps would be reduced to acceptable levels.

The individual skills track (so named since all 125 members of MI would participate, not just managers) was scheduled for three workshops: one full day in February, March, and April 1985. The first skills workshop would concentrate on improving people management and problem management skills, the second workshop would enable the participants to gain further experience with their new skills on a simulated MI project, and the third workshop would focus on additional ways in which to augment skills for addressing complex business problems. Again, in order to foster a safe learning environment, Salary I and II personnel would meet separately for group exercises and discussions.

During the first three months of the schedule, the first half of each month included a formal session in the culture track and the second half of the same month included a formal session in the skills track. This "dual tracking" seemed appropriate since the diagnostic interviews had revealed that MI members were quite open to learning, change, and improvement.

The team-building track was scheduled to reunite all Salary I and II personnel in their natural work groups for the first time during the improvement program. One all-day workshop was scheduled for May 1985, and subsequent monthly sessions would be scheduled as on-site meetings if necessary. (Since no troublemakers had been mentioned during the diagnostic interviews, no individual counseling sessions were scheduled.) The first team-building workshop would enable the members in each work group to synthesize the different cultural norms and sanctioning systems that had been developed in Salary I and Salary II subgroups during the prior tracks. Then members would make use of various team-building assessments to pinpoint and eliminate any barriers to effective group functioning. The next sessions would assess the progress being made on applying the new cultural norms and the new skills in all group discussions in the workplace; then action steps would be developed to overcome any remaining obstacles. If, after the third session, any *inter*group problems had not been resolved in the process, interteam-building workshops would be scheduled for the relevant groups.

The strategy-structure track was scheduled to begin with a one-day workshop in May 1985, after forming a problem management organization (PMO) of approximately fifteen members representing all levels and areas in MI. Since Kodak had just reorganized around a new strategy, the participants in this track would not be starting from scratch. Nevertheless, the diagnostic interviews had revealed considerable disagreement on the philosophy of market intelligence and how this philosophy should be translated into a mission statement, specific objectives, policies, and procedures throughout MI. The participants in this track were scheduled to meet once a month with the consultants and many more times on their own so that they could present their recommendations for strategy-structure improvements to Barabba and the MI directors by fall 1985.

The reward system track also was scheduled to begin with a one-day workshop in May 1985, since the basic parameters of MI's strategy and structure were known and only a fine tuning of these documents was required. The consultants would meet once a month with approximately fifteen participants representing all the levels and areas in MI—a different PMO from the one that was organized for the strategy-structure track. Between these scheduled meetings, participants in the reward system track would meet on their own in their collateral groups to address any reward system problems— revealed through the diagnostic results and subsequent experience. The participants would present their recommendations for reward system changes to Barabba and the MI directors by January 1986.

### Implementing the Tracks

Responsibility for the complete program's success was neither delegated to the consultants nor assigned to any staff group. Instead, the shadow track—a special steering committee composed of Barabba and the three directors of the business groups, plus an additional director who would coordinate the logistics of the program—was formed to manage the whole implementation process. As shown in Figure 22, the shadow track would run parallel to all five tracks. This group would monitor the program's progress and do whatever was necessary to ensure its success. Formal meetings, at least once per month, would be held by this group and would be attended periodically by the consultants.

### Starting with the Culture Track

The first track began, as scheduled, in February 1985. In the first part of the workshop, I presented an overview of the Barriers to Success model (Figure 3), a summary of the diagnostic results from all the interviews (only the directors had seen the report previously), and an outline of the five-track program that was scheduled for MI. Then the participants were asked to respond to the Myers-Briggs Type Indicator (Myers, 1962, 1978) in order to identify each individual's personality type (NF, NT, ST, or SF). Following a lecture on personality and culture, the participants individually responded to two forms of the Kilmann-Saxton Culture-Gap Survey (1983): (1) actual and desired norms *within* the MI community; (2) actual and desired norms *between* MI and the client organizations (the LOBs in the three business groups). These two perspectives reflected the matrix organization for MI members who were working simultaneously for an MI director and a Kodak manager—as shown previously in Figure 21. (Those MI members who were not in a matrix relationship, of course, completed only one form of the survey.)

Once the participants scored their four culture-gaps (Task Support, Task Innovation, Social Relationships, and Personal Freedom—see Chapter Three) for inside MI and outside MI, they calculated the average culture-gaps for their subgroup (separated by Salary I and II personnel). Using these results as background information, the participants then listed actual and desired norms within their subgroup and toward others (the rest of MI and their LOB clients). Next each subgroup developed its own sanctioning system. The first workshop in the culture track concluded that participants should meet on their own during the next month in order to finalize their plans for cultural change. Each subgroup also was asked to prepare a written assignment: (1) List the actual and desired norms for behavior within your subgroup and toward others; (2) what will happen when a victory occurs (a desired norm is enacted) and when a violation occurs (a dysfunctional norm is enacted)?

*Beginning the Skills Track and*
*Continuing with the Culture Track*

Later in February, as scheduled, the second track began with an all-day workshop on people management and problem management skills. An interpersonal ice-breaking exercise was the first activity of the day. The diagnostic interviews, remember, had revealed that MI members did not know one another very well and thought their interpersonal relationships were too aloof. To eliminate this barrier to open communication and information sharing, each participant was asked to write on easel-pad paper his responses to these items: name, education, hometown, hobbies and outside interests, goals and aspirations, greatest accomplishment, greatest disappointment, and an idol or hero. Each person was then given two pieces of masking tape so that his completed paper could be taped to his shoulders. Next the participants spent an hour walking around the room and getting to know one another through this initially awkward, but eventually enriching, experience. After this exercise, everyone removed his paper and hung the unusual artifact on the wall of the classroom.

Following the ice-breaking exercise, several hours were devoted to developing skills for managing people and groups. Several topics were covered: blind areas of one's personality and behavior, ego strength and self-worth, principles for giving and receiving effective feedback, how to communicate in nondefensive ways, different models of motivation, different modes of managing conflict, different styles of leadership, and principles for effective group process. Numerous concepts were discussed, several personality instruments were administered, and a few group exercises were conducted so that participants could use these theories and methods on the job. Then, using a business case, the five steps of problem management were illustrated along with the various methods for conducting assumptional analysis. The first skills workshop concluded with the second written assignment for each subgroup: (1) List all the critical principles that were learned during the day, (2) develop action plans to apply these principles back on the job, and (3) plan some dramatic act to illustrate your commitment to using these principles in the workplace.

In the months to come, participants in the program would frequently refer to this first skills workshop as an "action-packed day." Not only did they recall the strange ice-breaking event, but on numerous occasions they even cited the business case and other learning exercises. Whenever a meeting wandered off course, for example, members would make reference to a particular group exercise by declaring: "We're lost at sea again!" Thus a new common language and a shared conceptual understanding gradually spread throughout the MI organization. As personality types and cultural norms became part of MI's vocabulary, members began perceiving, thinking, and behaving differently on the job.

In early March, the second workshop in the culture track took place. The steps of problem management—with assumptional analysis—were used to convey *why* culture-gaps do not close just from talking about them and *how* the sanctioning system can be used to break old cultural habits and reinforce adaptive behavior. The third workshop in the culture track, conducted in early April, continued with this problem management approach to closing culture-gaps.

In late March, the second workshop in the skills track took place. This session gave participants another opportunity to practice their skills for problem management by working on a realistic simulation of a client requesting a study from MI. (This hypothetical project was developed by the shadow track especially for this workshop.) One of the group MI directors, Marv McNeice, introduced the project to the participants and then played the role of client throughout the day. While the group members did an excellent job of applying many of the principles they had learned in the previous skills workshop, a key experience occurred: Once the scope of the project was outlined, very few groups asked McNeice to meet with them and explain his needs and objectives more thoroughly. In fact, it was surprising to see McNeice walking from group to group without being approached for further clarification or being asked for more information—both of which he was prepared to provide upon request. In some groups, the members even asked McNeice to leave the room so they could concentrate on the project without his interference!

At the end of the simulation, McNeice asked why so few groups had taken advantage of his—the client's—presence. At first the groups were defensive as they realized they had resorted to the self-contained posture that had dominated Kodak for decades; then, with further discussion, they agreed that a powerful lesson had been learned: MI must interact with its LOB clients continually so that its market research studies would satisfy client needs—an important criterion for successful problem management in a service organization.

### Understanding and Managing Time

By early April, a recurring complaint began to gain momentum in MI: Because of all the pressure from the new LOBs to obtain vital market information, many MI members felt they no longer had the time to attend the workshops. It seemed that the LOBs were in a crisis mode and were expecting market intelligence to provide all the answers to their overwhelming number of business questions. During a meeting of the shadow track, I reminded the directors that the diagnostic interviews had revealed that members felt a strong cultural pressure to be busy at all times and work long hours until exhaustion. Although members said this style of work was basic to Kodak (and consistent with the Protestant work ethic), I was beginning to wonder whether the recent surge in complaints stemmed from deficient skills in managing time—rather than from an increase in the workload per se. And perhaps this skill deficiency was coming to the forefront now because the new competitive world was being confronted for the first time.

Some directors in the shadow track argued that the best way to solve the time problem was to cancel the improvement program: The extra time saved would help MI conduct the vast number of

market research studies being requested by the new LOBs. Barabba
listened intently and then insisted that it was not acceptable to
terminate the improvement effort—especially not now, when MI
seemed to need it the most. Besides, he argued, the full benefits of
the program would not be realized unless the fourth and fifth tracks
were implemented.

After more discussion, a compromise solution was proposed
by the directors who were most concerned about alleviating the
immediate work pressures: All the remaining sessions in the
program, which had been scheduled from 8:30 A.M. to 4:00 P.M.,
would be rescheduled from 8:00 A.M. to 2:00 P.M. with a forty-five-
minute working lunch. In this way, several directors thought the
participants could return to their offices in the afternoon for several
more hours of work. I agreed that the new schedule would provide
sufficient—but not ideal—time to keep the program on course. But
I proposed that the third workshop in the individual skills track
(April 1985) should concentrate exclusively on the principles and
practice of time management. Such a switch in content seemed
justified given the LOB pressures on MI. The shadow track agreed
that the improvement program should proceed with these adjustments in both schedule and content.

Following this meeting with the shadow track, I had to
remind myself of two fantasies I used to cherish regarding the
internal support and external dynamics surrounding a long-term
improvement effort—that the whole top management group would
provide complete, unanimous, and continuing support throughout
the entire program and that no outside events would ever interfere
with the scheduled plans for implementation. In reality, commitment to an improvement effort—especially one that is central to the
functioning of the organization—is always a matter of degree and a
question of getting wholehearted acceptance from the key members.
Since the organization's setting is always changing—especially with
today's dynamic complexity—the program's implementation must
adapt to these realities and *proceed*, so long as the necessary
conditions for success are still evident. Determinations of the critical
thresholds of acceptance and the necessary conditions for success,
however, are subjective decisions that, one hopes, are made for the

right reasons using the right criteria: What will enhance organizational success?

In late April, the special six-hour workshop on time management struck a chord with most of the members in MI and proved to be one of their most valuable sessions. Following a lecture on time management and external and internal control, each participant in the workshop was asked to develop four lists: (1) the tasks she should be spending *more* time on, (2) the tasks she should be spending *less* time on, (3) the time-wasters causing these time-gaps that she *could* directly control, and (4) the time-wasters that she *could not* directly control in her immediate workplace. After discussing these lists in their subgroups, the participants came to a startling conclusion: *They waste most of their time.* The participants realized that wasting time occurs in several ways: (1) working without a clear sense of priorities or without sufficient planning, (2) not working on the most important projects first and the least important projects last, (3) jumping from one task or project to another before bringing anything to completion, (4) allowing unannounced visits and telephone calls to interrupt concentration throughout the day, (5) not being able to say no to requests that are peripheral and really pertain to someone else's job, and (6) not having an agenda *before* all group meetings and not sticking to that agenda during all group discussions.

The experience the participants had of openly discussing all their time-wasters and time-gaps was much like discussing cultural norms or hidden assumptions: It enabled group members to gain control of unconscious choices that interfered with performance and morale. At the end of the day, the participants were given their third written assignment of the improvement program. Each subgroup was asked to summarize its conclusions on time-wasters and to propose solutions and action plans for closing its time-gaps.

Since this workshop on time management occurred after several months of dual tracking with the culture and skills workshops, the members in MI were able to apply their new knowledge quite readily back on the job. Not only was the culture already changing to support new ways of doing things, but the skills for communicating intentions more assertively were being evidenced both within and between work groups. Thus it was much easier now for members to say no—courteously, of course—and to insist that job priorities either had to be respected outright or had to be renegotiated.

### Proceeding with the Team-Building Track

The third track began, as scheduled, in May 1985. The process of reuniting the Salary I and II subgroups into their natural MI work groups for the first time during the improvement program went smoothly. In the previous month, many members commented that the first-class/second-class distinction between Salary I and Salary II personnel was fading. Managers and professionals (Salary II) developed—and enforced—these desired norms: Everyone in Kodak deserves equal respect; everyone should be viewed as a resource for defining and solving complex problems; don't support class distinctions in the workplace. Clerical and technical personnel (Salary I) developed—and enforced—these desired norms: Assert yourself in a supportive and confident way; professional respect comes from professional behavior; keep up to date on MI projects so that you understand the context of your own contributions; participate in educational and training opportunities that will improve your value to the organization. Thus the first topic in the team-building track—synthesizing cultural norms and sanctioning systems in Salary I and Salary II subgroups—was rather easy since MI already had overcome its status barriers to organizational success.

The next step in the team-building track was to assess team-gaps. On seven-point scales (1 = not at all; 7 = extremely so), indicating an O for actual and an X for desired, each member responded to items like these: To what extent do you feel a real part of your team? To what extent do you understand your team's goals? How well does your team manage its time by establishing priorities and procedures for choosing among competing projects and activities? How effective is your team at involving outside people when you need additional resources or expertise? How effective is your team at monitoring and adapting to your clients' needs for market information? Each natural work group then calculated its average team-gaps—the differences between actual and desired scores on fifteen dimensions of work-group functioning.

Identifying team-gaps, according to this quantitative assessment, is much like sensing problems—the initial step of problem management. In the remainder of the first team-building session, each natural work group focused its efforts on defining the problems underlying its five largest team-gaps, deriving solutions to these problems, and planning for the implementation of solutions back at the workplace. Much of the discussion in these work groups touched on earlier conversations on cultural norms and individual skills. Now, however, the emphasis was not on learning new material but on applying both the new culture and the new skills day after day. Thus the team-building track concerned *why* all the new material was not being applied and *what* could be done about it. This session ended with the fourth written assignment of the improvement program. Each work group was asked to summarize its team-gaps, the root causes of these gaps, and the specific steps that would be taken to bring these gaps within acceptable levels.

Following the first team-building workshop, each work group was asked to appoint a process observer (PO) before the start of every meeting at the workplace. This person would monitor the quality of the group process according to a number of "process helps" (developed by the shadow track) and then, at the end of the meeting, would provide constructive feedback to the group. Table 1 summarizes MI's criteria for a successful meeting—including premeeting and postmeeting activities.

In subsequent team-building sessions, the natural work groups continued their efforts at reducing team-gaps with their new improved skills in people and problem management. In numerous cases, I was invited to a group's regular business meeting to observe the process and give members my critique. After several months of these on-site activities, I could see that most of the work groups were applying the basic material they had learned during the first two tracks. I could also see that the use of "process helps" and process observers ensured that each team would continue to monitor and improve its functioning of its own volition.

### Table 1. "Process Helps" for Successful Meetings.

Planning the Meeting
1.  What are the primary objectives of the meeting?
2.  Is there an alternative to a meeting (for example, a phone call, a letter, or a visit)?
3.  What process should be used for addressing each objective?
4.  Who should attend the meeting? Who has the relevant information and expertise? Who has a stake in the outcome of the decision? Who has vastly different views on the topic?
5.  When should you hold the meeting? Where, how long, how big a room, and what equipment is needed?
6.  What could go wrong? What are you going to do about it?
7.  Is a premeeting or pre-information in order? Does everyone know what he needs to bring to the meeting and why he was invited?
8.  What is the agenda? An agenda should be provided for every meeting—even before the meeting if possible.

Conducting the Meeting
1.  At the start of each meeting, designate one person as the process observer (PO). The PO will make certain that the meeting stays on track. *Every member* of the group, however, should be monitoring the group's process as well.
2.  Make the objectives of the meeting visible to each person.
3.  Have an agenda showing the objectives *and the time allotted for each.* (If an agenda has not been prepared, take time to do so; but develop the whole agenda before any item is discussed—items do not usually emerge in the order of their priority! Next, prioritize the agenda items and decide what should be accomplished by the end of the meeting.)
4.  Define problems before attempting to solve them. Is there another way of defining the problem—based on a different viewpoint—that will facilitate a solution and its implementation?
5.  Apply the principles of time management at all times! Discuss items in their order of importance, stick to the most important item until some resolution is achieved, then move on to the next item of importance, and so forth. Do not dwell on topics that do not contribute to the established objectives of the meeting.
6.  The culture of the group should encourage risk taking, different viewpoints, creativity, innovation—since *any* new approach is typically a minority position. Draw out the quiet members of the group. Get nervous if the group arrives at a quick consensus on a complex problem.
7.  Only one conversation should be taking place at a time. Listen carefully to what is being said. Everyone should pause to allow others to enter the conversation.
8.  Stop periodically to assess the quality of the group's process. Is the meeting proceeding on course? Should the agenda or the schedule be changed?

Table 1. "Process Helps" for Successful Meetings, Cont'd.

9. Someone should take responsibility for documenting the key points of discussion, decisions made, and actions recommended.

Closing the Meeting
1. Prepare a complete list of action items established at the meeting, a description of the task, the person responsible, and the due date. This information should be summarized as a "To Do List."
2. Determine the agenda for the next meeting—objectives to be accomplished and so on. The agenda should include following up on the action items from the previous meeting.
3. Do not adjourn the meeting until the PO has reported on the quality of the group's process. Get everyone's opinion: How did we do? What can we improve? Did we accomplish the objectives?

### Conducting the Strategy-Structure Track

The fourth track began in July 1985, two months later than scheduled. The increase in market research studies requested by the LOB managers had created a demanding workload for all MI members. Now it was even more important to manage time with an effective group. Despite all this busyness, though, sixteen members representing all the areas and levels in MI met with the consultants for one full day in order to begin the process of defining and solving MI's strategy-structure problems.

In their problem management organization (PMO), participants in the strategy-structure track went back to the basics: What *is* strategy and what *is* structure? What do these documents provide for organizational members? Why are these documents needed in different forms to help different people working on different tasks with different objectives in mind? What is MI's current strategy-structure arrangement? Where is MI headed in the next five years? How can MI's strategy and structure be fine-tuned for the future?

The sixteen participants thus were exposed to most of the basic concepts of organizational strategy and structure presented in Chapter Six. Then the strategy-structure problems that were identified during the diagnostic interviews were reviewed. Next Barabba presented MI's five-year vision along with an explicit statement of what is open or closed territory for discussion.

Participants could not question the reorganization of Kodak into lines of business—this was out of their hands. Nor could they question Kodak's strategic mission of becoming the world's premier imaging and information systems company. But apart from these constraints there was a lot of room for strategy-structure improvements in MI—particularly with regard to the documentation each member would have at his or her disposal. Participants were also free to recommend just how MI's own strategic mission should be stated and what structural improvements could add efficiency and effectiveness to its operations.

Following the various presentations and discussions on all the introductory material, the remainder of this first workshop focused on the critical issues—problems and opportunities—associated with strategy and structure. A community discussion among all the participants revealed three basic themes: macrodesign, microdesign, and links and flows. The sixteen participants then formed three subgroups to work on these sets of problems. A coordinating group was established with a representative from each of the three subgroups. Its purpose was to coordinate the various task flows among the three groups, to communicate with the rest of MI about the progress of the strategy-structure track, and to synthesize and present the final recommendations to the shadow track.

The subgroup on macrodesign would reformulate a concise statement of MI's mission with recommendations about MI's formal structure and the mission of each of its subunits. The subgroup on microdesign would develop a system of procedures to ensure that personnel know their fundamental purpose in the organization and the means at their disposal for being successful. The subgroup on links and flows would prepare a list of critical communication, information management, and external relations needs within MI worldwide and would then recommend a process for satisfying these needs.

During the summer and fall of 1985, the participants met frequently in their three subgroups to define and solve their set of strategy-structure problems. On most issues, they sought the advice of other members in MI who were not involved in this track. When more systematic information was desired, they relied on their expert knowledge of conducting market research studies in order to survey the opinions of all MI members with structured questionnaires.

In November 1985, the coordinating group presented its recommendations for strategy-structure changes to the shadow track. The following items highlight the key recommendations: MI should provide not only information but also the necessary resources, tools, and expertise so that Kodak decision makers can make effective use of that information; in order to fulfill its mission, MI must state the *implications* of the information it gathers for LOB decision makers; MI's clients should be helped to define their information needs; and since these needs go beyond market information, market intelligence is really *business* intelligence—and the function should be renamed accordingly.

Other recommendations were offered by the participants in the strategy-structure track. Each new person, upon joining MI, should receive an employee orientation package and a copy of MI's standard operating procedures. Whenever possible, a mentor should be assigned to help the new person with on-the-job training and general coaching. Management should be more proactive in its support of employee participation in training programs. Project assignments should be made to broaden the employee's skills and knowledge across product/market areas rather than to develop experts in very limited jobs. Group MI directors should communicate more fully among themselves and with MI personnel about position openings; all job openings should be posted publicly and mention the essential qualifications for job success. Two documents were recommended for all MI personnel. One would be the traditional job description, a general statement describing, for example, what an MI analyst does. The other document would be called a position guide—an informal contract of performance expectations agreed to by the supervisor and the employee. Job descriptions should be kept in a central file and be made available to MI's members at their request.

In the following months, the shadow track met to review all these recommendations and prepare a response to the MI community: Which items would be implemented as stated? Which items would be modified before being implemented? Which recommendations would not be implemented in any form? In each case, the reasons behind the decision would be stated explicitly. Within one year, the great majority of recommendations were implemented—often without modification—since understanding and acceptance had been built into the process of developing solutions to strategy-structure barriers to success.

### Conducting the Reward System Track

The fifth track, scheduled to begin in May, was postponed for several months. Similar to the case of the strategy-structure track, the delay was due in part to the vast number of market research studies being requested by the new LOBs. But in the case of the reward system track, there was another cause for delay: Some members in the shadow track—the Group MI directors—did not want to relinquish their prerogative to manage the reward system. What began as a reasonable concern about choosing the right members for the PMO became an exercise in choosing the *perfect* set of people to represent MI's full range of interests. After several months of debating why one person would be a better representative than another, I finally lost patience: "So what if the composition of the PMO is not perfect? Let's get on with the process and expand the membership later if we discover any serious deficiencies!" To this statement, one Group MI director responded: "If I'm not involved in this process and other people several levels below me are, my subordinates will know more about the intricate technical details of the reward system than I do. That's not right."

At this point I reminded the directors in the shadow track that the participants in the reward system track would be making *recommendations*, not decisions, and there would be ample opportunity for everyone to learn the details of the system. In fact, the whole decision process would help everyone understand the reward system much better than before. Eventually, the members of the shadow track surrendered to reality: The diagnostic results had revealed numerous barriers stemming from the design and adminis-tration of the current reward system that only a participative process could hope to remove.

Before proceeding with the fifth track, there was another critical issue to resolve: What could be changed and what was fixed with regard to Kodak's formal reward system? In July 1985, a memo from Chairman Colby Chandler informed all senior executives that, by January 1986, a Special Recognition Plan was to be designed and implemented by each organizational unit. In August 1985, MI was informed that Kodak was revamping its formal reward system and all units should postpone making suggestions on improving the system until the new one was developed. Consequently, the shadow track agreed that participants in the reward system track should concentrate on developing the Special Recognition Plan (SRP) for application to the unique circumstances in MI—which is exactly what Colby Chandler was asking each organization in Kodak to do. This focus certainly restricted the scope of the improvement program, especially since numerous barriers to success pertained to the company-wide reward system. But the shadow track agreed that, once the new system was announced, the reward system track would be reinstated to examine how MI could modify and adapt the new system to its specific needs.

Naturally, I felt disappointed that the fifth track would focus on just one aspect of the whole reward system. But the realities of organizational life often preclude the literal translation of theory into practice. Nonetheless, I was convinced that the reward system track could make a significant contribution by designing and implementing—with imagination and enthusiasm—a Special Recognition Plan.

### Will a Change in Leadership Stop the Improvement Program?

In September, just one month before the reward system track was to begin, Barabba informed me that he would be leaving Eastman Kodak to join General Motors as executive director of its equivalent of market intelligence. I was concerned. How would this change in leadership affect the improvement program? After all, Barabba had played a major role in initiating the program and moving it along. He assured me, however, that he fully expected the program to continue. Top management and the MI directors would not allow the program's many benefits to be undermined, regardless of the previous debates about when and how the various tracks of the program should be implemented. While I was not entirely convinced by his arguments, I did have to admit that, thus far, he had predicted correctly the outcome of all the other critical events.

In early October, Kodak announced that Bill Lawton, the director of International MI, would replace Barabba as director of the company's entire market intelligence function. Lawton telephoned me to discuss his new job and assure me the program would continue as planned, without interruption. He affirmed his support of the improvement effort and said he intended to take full advantage of what the program was providing for MI as well as for Kodak.

On the following day, I had another opportunity to discuss MI's change in leadership with Barabba. And I began to see that Lawton's appointment as head of MI had a lot to do with the fact that his management style so consistently reflected the principles and practices of the program. In all likelihood, selecting Lawton to head MI had sent a message to every member that not only would the program be completed but MI had achieved sufficient credibility in its own right to survive its first leader. In the members' eyes, Kodak's top management had made the right leadership decision for MI's future and for the benefit of its LOB clients.

### Returning to the Reward System Track

In mid-October, a group of fifteen participants—representing every level and area in MI—met in an all-day workshop to learn about the purpose and functioning of reward systems and special recognition plans. They were exposed to most of the basic concepts presented in Chapter Seven: What is motivation, what is performance, what is measurement, what is a reward, and how does the organization motivate high performance—measured objectively—with its extrinsic and intrinsic rewards? Next they reviewed the reward system problems that were identified during the diagnostic interviews. Lawton then presented the guidelines of the Special Recognition Plan (SRP), as outlined by the top management, and explained why the participants had to delay an analysis of the total reward system.

After presentation and discussion of all the introductory materials, this workshop focused on the critical issues—problems and opportunities—associated with developing and implementing an effective special recognition plan. A community discussion among all the participants revealed three basic themes: design, implementation, and review. The fifteen participants then formed three subgroups to work on these sets of problems. A coordinating group was formed with a representative from each of the three subgroups.

The subgroup on design would develop the reward criteria and procedures for the SRP; the subgroup on implementation would determine how to translate the plan into practice; the subgroup on review would determine how the SRP's design and implementation should be monitored and adjusted for different areas, levels, and situations in MI.

During the next few months, from October through December 1985, the participants met frequently in their three subgroups as they worked to define and solve their set of reward system problems. In December, a preliminary plan was presented to most of MI's members via focused group interviews. Based on their reactions, the SRP was revised by the participants in the reward system track and then presented to the shadow track in early January 1986. Without any further modifications, the SRP was approved by the shadow track and was implemented later that same month.

While there is no need here to describe every aspect of the SRP, a few of its key features can be summarized. First, a special "rewards review committee" would be formed to ensure that the plan's implementation would be effective. This committee would meet periodically to review the documented "recognitions" and determine whether the plan is meeting the company's objectives. The committee would also consider whether the plan is being administered fairly, would take note of any emerging problems, and would offer suggestions for improvement. This committee would be composed of representative members from different levels and areas in MI. Annually, the committee would survey MI personnel in order to solicit their comments and attitudes toward the SRP in practice.

All MI employees are eligible for recognition in the SRP program. Since awards under this plan are meant to recognize efforts or achievements that significantly exceed the expected norm for the individual or the group, they are separate from the performance appraisal process. Awards should not be used to fund events unrelated to performance. Directors, incidentally, are eligible only if they are recommended for recognition by their subordinates. (The recommendation must be made to the director's superior.)

Furthermore, the SRP specifies that recognition can be informal, tangible, cash, or any combination of these types. Informal recognition may be a simple thank you, a handshake, a special visit from a manager—or assignment to a special project or a greater degree of independence. Tangible recognition may be a note or letter of thanks, a certificate, a plaque, a luncheon or dinner, tickets for special events, or a memento such as a pen or key ring. Cash recognition may be an award of $150 to $500 based on the significance of the accomplishment. Ordinarily, no more than about 10 percent of the members in a large unit in MI would receive cash recognition in a given year. Recommendations for special recognition can be made by a first-line supervisor (coordinator) or director. Tangible and cash rewards require the approval of a business unit or divisional director. Finally, recognition should be given as soon as possible after completion of the event. Presentation of awards may be informal or formal.

## Evaluating the Results

In January 1986, my involvement with the improvement program ceased. From this point on, it was expected that MI could implement its strategy-structure and reward system changes without outside help. Furthermore, if new problems or opportunities arose, MI had the culture and skills to mobilize a new PMO on its own initiative.

Two years later, in February 1988, I called Bill Lawton to see if I would be allowed to present the Eastman Kodak story in this book. He was very enthusiastic about the prospect and suggested I visit Kodak to discuss the results of the improvement program with the members themselves. In fact, he would schedule two focused group meetings with the members of Business Research (the new name for the old Market Intelligence). The first group would consist of members who had actually participated in the improvement program from beginning to end; the second group would consist of members who had entered Business Research during the past year, though they had worked for other units in the company. Lawton thought it would be interesting to see how the two groups viewed the results of the program. I agreed. If the improvement effort was successful, the second group should have internalized the principles and practices of the program through socialization and the pressures of the new culture.

In March 1988, I spent a day with Business Research. In the morning I met with five members from different areas who had been through the completely integrated program—from late 1984 to early 1986. I learned several interesting things from this group. First, if I suggested today that an improvement program should separate Salary I from Salary II personnel, there would be an uproar. Apparently a strong bond of loyalty and respect had developed between these two former classes of citizenship. This first group offered several examples—with considerable pride—showing the fundamental and equal contribution that both secretaries and other members provide in the same organization. Or as one person put it: "We even have a career path outlined for secretaries, which probably doesn't exist in any other organization in Kodak."

Second, there seems to be a corporate-wide acceptance of Business Research, not just by top management. In the old days (three years ago), as one member suggested, the new heads of the business units viewed MI as having people with analytical skills but not "street smarts." For the LOB managers, being asked to use market information to inform decisions before the fact—rather than to justify decisions after the fact—was quite at variance with traditional practice. Thus MI, as had been revealed through the diagnostic interviews with clients, was often seen as a nuisance and a place to send analytical marketing people who had not worked out in the real world of customers and sales. Now, however, the tide had turned. The term "street smarts" was no longer in vogue; in fact, the term now suggested an untrained mind. Above all, Business Research today was being viewed as an *ideal* job experience for the future business managers in the LOBs. Indeed, in the past three years 50 percent of the personnel from the old MI function had been lured away to work directly for the LOB managers. Why? *Because of* their analytical understanding of customers and the marketplace.

Business Research's problem was to hold on to their personnel long enough to train them before they were snatched up by the LOBs.

That afternoon, I met with the second focused group composed of four members who had entered Business Research after the formal activities of the improvement program had concluded. This meeting turned out to be the most enlightening experience of the day. Since Lawton had not told this group what would be discussed, I began by asking them what they knew about the five-track program. They responded: "What are the five tracks?" Taken aback by this response, I tried a different tack by asking them what they knew about the "Kilmann process," the phrase often used to identify the program. They responded: "We heard that it had something to do with culture, but that's about it. As a matter of fact, we don't even know the purpose of this meeting or why we were chosen to discuss something we know nothing about." I was in a state of shock. My first thought was that the program neither was internalized nor had been passed on to the new members. They did not even know who I was!

Once again I tried a different approach to soliciting reactions to the program. This time I simply asked them what life was like in Business Research and how it compared with their experiences in the rest of the company. Finally, I had hit upon the right question and the discussion came to life: "This is the most cohesive organization I've ever experienced. When you first begin working in other parts of Kodak, they give you a desk and that's about it. Several months later they let you know what's going on and what's expected. Here, I was assigned a mentor, taken to lunch, walked around to meet people, and given a complete orientation package to learn about the organization, its mission, and its procedures." After more comments were offered along these lines, I described the purpose of the five-track program and talked about cultural norms, individual skills, and team spirit. Their reaction to my summary was: "You've just described what we experienced in Business Research from Day One."

Another person in the focused group responded: "There's something different around here. You can feel it. Something happened to this part of the organization that has not been experienced in other parts of Kodak. People are warm, friendly, and they really care about you. There's an enthusiasm and an excitement in this place that is contagious. Secretaries, for example, are involved in everything that goes on. They initiate activities and plan special events. They're highly respected and admired. What is most uncanny in Business Research is that we have no trouble communicating across areas and gaining cooperation from other groups when needed. We never before experienced this kind of work environment in Kodak."

When I asked this group about the problems they encounter in Business Research, one member replied: "The reward system doesn't support team efforts and the system of grades is out of date and confusing." With surprise, I asked about the Special Recognition Plan. The response was: "Oh, that part of the reward system works great. People often get praise and awards soon after some important project has been completed. We even have ceremonies and parties to celebrate our accomplishments. It's the performance appraisal system that is archaic." I then remembered that the fifth track was not permitted to address the formal reward system—only the Special Recognition Plan could be designed by MI. Other comments suggested that Kodak had never altered the company-wide reward system as planned. Not surprisingly, therefore, only the SRP was motivating high performance and sustaining all improvements.

At the end of the day, I left Kodak with a fascinating discovery: Those members of Business Research who had arrived after the formal steps of the improvement program were conducted had never heard of me or the five tracks. Yet they were living proof that the program has had a lasting impact on the functioning of the organization. Ultimately it is organizational success, not names of people or programs, that signifies the achievement of a long-term improvement effort.

## The Bottom Line

The completely integrated program at Eastman Kodak proved to be a worthwhile experience for both members and consultants. The conditions for success were evident in the very beginning: Barabba, the director of Market Intelligence, understood the process of planned change and the sequence of five tracks. He also had sufficient commitment to proceed from Kodak's top management and was prepared to do whatever it took to implement the program amidst a major reorganization and increasing pressures for bottom-line results. Lawton, who took over Barabba's job just before the fifth track was initiated, repeatedly demonstrated his commitment to see the whole program through. Although numerous modifications to the original schedule were made during the implementation stage, all decisions on the content and conduct of the program were guided by the diagnostic stage and by the evolving needs of the organization. This ongoing adaptability keeps the program vibrant and relevant to all key stakeholders—which, essentially, is just what the organization itself must do in order to create and maintain organizational success.

# Bibliography

Allen, R. F. "The Ik in the Office." *Organizational Dynamics,* Winter 1980, pp. 26–41.

Allen, R. F., and Dyer, F. "A Tool for Tapping the Organizational Unconscious." *Personnel Journal,* March 1980, pp. 192–198.

Allen, R. F., and Kraft, C. *The Organizational Unconscious: How to Create the Corporate Culture You Want and Need.* Englewood Cliffs, N.J.: Prentice-Hall, 1982.

Allenbaugh, G. E. "Coaching: A Management Tool for a More Effective Work Performance." *Management Review,* May 1983, pp. 21–26.

Argyris, C. *Intervention Theory and Method: A Behavioral Science View.* Reading, Mass.: Addison-Wesley, 1970.

Asch, S. E. "Opinions and Social Pressure." *Scientific American,* Nov. 1955, pp. 31–34.

Atkinson, J. W. (ed.). *Motives in Fantasy, Action, and Society: A Method of Assessment and Study.* New York: Van Nostrand, 1958.

Barabba, V. P. "How Kodak's Market Intelligence System Cuts Risk, Speeds Decisions." *Management Review,* Aug. 1984, pp. 8–13.

Beer, M. *Organization Change and Development.* Santa Monica, Calif.: Goodyear, 1980.

Benét, S. V. *John Brown's Body.* New York: Holt, Rinehart & Winston, 1927.

Bennis, W. G. *Changing Organizations.* New York: McGraw-Hill, 1966.

Bennis, W. G., Benne, K. D., and Chin, R. *The Planning of Change.* (3rd ed.) New York: Holt, Rinehart & Winston, 1976.

Blake, R. R., Mouton, J. S., and Sloma, R. L. "The Union-Management Intergroup Laboratory: Strategy for Resolving Intergroup Conflict." *Journal of Applied Behavioral Science,* 1965, *1* (1), 25–57.

Bowen, D. D., and Kilmann, R. H. "Developing a Comparative Measure of the Learning Climate in Professional Schools." *Journal of Applied Psychology,* 1975, *60* (1), 71–79.

Boyle, R. J. "Designing the Energetic Organization: How a Honeywell Unit Stimulated Change and Innovation." *Management Review,* Aug. 1983, pp. 20–25.

Bramson, R. M. *Coping with Difficult People.* New York: Ballantine, 1981.

Capra, F. "The Turning Point: A New Vision of Reality." *The Futurist,* Dec. 1982, pp. 19–24.

Chakravarty, S. N., and Simon, R. "Has the World Passed Kodak By?" *Forbes,* Nov. 5, 1984, pp. 184–191.

Churchman, C. W. *The Design of Inquiring Systems.* New York: Basic Books, 1971.

"Conversation with Edson W. Spencer and Foster A. Boyle." *Organizational Dynamics,* Spring 1983, pp. 30–45.

"Corporate Culture: The Hard-to-Change Values That Spell Success or Failure." *Business Week,* Oct. 27, 1980, pp. 148–160.

Covin, T. J., and Kilmann, R. H. "Occupational Frame of Reference and the Identification of Critical Issues in Large-Scale Change Efforts." *Consultation,* forthcoming.

Davis, S. M., and Lawrence, P. R. *Matrix.* Reading, Mass.: Addison-Wesley, 1977.

Day, G. "Gaining Insights Through Strategic Analysis." *Journal of Business Strategy*, 1983, *4* (1), 51–58.

de Board, R. *The Psychoanalysis of Organizations*. London: Tavistock, 1978.

Deal, T. E., and Kennedy, A. A. *Corporate Cultures: The Rites and Rituals of Corporate Life*. Reading, Mass.: Addison-Wesley, 1982.

Dessler, G. *Personnel Management*. Reston, Va.: Reston Publishing, 1978.

"Detroit's Merry-Go-Round." *Business Week*, Sept. 12, 1983, pp. 72–81.

Deutsch, C. H. "Kodak Pays the Price for Change." *New York Times*, Mar. 6, 1988.

Diamond, M. A., and Allcorn, S. "Psychological Barriers to Personal Responsibility." *Organizational Dynamics*, Spring 1984, pp. 66–77.

Dollard, J., and Miller, N. E. *Personality and Psychotherapy: An Analysis in Terms of Learning, Thinking, and Culture*. New York: McGraw-Hill, 1950.

Downs, A. *Inside Bureaucracy*. Boston: Little, Brown, 1967.

Dyer, W. G. *Team Building: Issues and Alternatives*. Reading, Mass.: Addison-Wesley, 1977.

Emshoff, J. R., Mitroff, I. I., and Kilmann, R. H. "The Role of Idealization in Long Range Planning: An Essay on the Logical and Social-Emotional Aspects of Planning." *Technological Forecasting and Social Change*, 1978, *11* (4), 335–348.

Ewing, D. W. "How to Negotiate with Employee Objectors." *Harvard Business Review*, Jan.-Feb. 1983, pp. 103–110.

Fenichel, O. *The Psychoanalytic Theory of Neurosis*. New York: Norton, 1972.

Flax, S. "The Ten Toughest Bosses in America." *Fortune*, Aug. 6, 1984, pp. 18–23.

French, W. L., and Bell, C. H. *Organization Development: Behavioral Science Interventions for Organization Improvement*. Englewood Cliffs, N.J.: Prentice-Hall, 1978.

Galbraith, J. *Designing Complex Organizations*. Reading, Mass.: Addison-Wesley, 1973.

Gelfman, M. "The Role of Irresponsibility in Obsessive-

Compulsive Neurosis." *Contemporary Psychoanalysis,* 1970, 7 (1), 36-47.

Gibson, J. L., Ivancevich, J. M., and Donnelly, J. H., Jr. *Organizations: Behavior, Structure, Processes.* (6th ed.) Dallas: Business Publications, 1988.

Gittler, H. "One More Panacea and We'll All Go Nuts." *Industry Week,* Mar. 4, 1985, pp. 98, 104-105.

Hackman, J. R., and Oldham, G. R. *Work Redesign.* Reading, Mass.: Addison-Wesley, 1980.

Hax, A. C., and Majluf, N. S. "Organization Design: A Case Study on Matching Strategy and Structure." *Journal of Business Strategy,* 1983, *4* (2), 72-86.

Hayes, R. H., and Abernathy, W. J. "Managing Our Way to Economic Decline." *Harvard Business Review,* July-Aug. 1980, pp. 67-77.

Hinrichs, J. R. "Avoid the 'Quick Fix' Approach to Productivity Problems." *Personnel Administrator,* July 1983, pp. 39-43.

Huse, E. F. *Organization Development and Change.* (2nd ed.) St. Paul, Minn.: West, 1980.

Jung, C. G. *Psychological Types.* Boston: Routledge & Kegan Paul, 1923.

Kanter, R. M. "Change Masters and the Intricate Architecture of Corporate Culture Change." *Management Review,* Oct. 1983, pp. 18-28.

Kaplan, J. M., and Kaplan, E. E. "Organizational Restructuring: How Managers Can Actively Assist in Shaping a Firm's New Architecture." *Management Review,* Jan. 1984, pp. 15-21.

Katz, D., and Kahn, R. L. *The Social Psychology of Organizations.* New York: Wiley, 1966.

Kets de Vries, M.F.R., and Miller, D. *The Neurotic Organization: Diagnosing and Changing Counterproductive Styles of Management.* San Francisco: Jossey-Bass, 1984.

Kilmann, R. H. "The Effect of Interpersonal Values on Laboratory Training: An Empirical Investigation." *Human Relations,* 1974a, *27* (3), 247-265.

Kilmann, R. H. "An Organic-Adaptive Organization: The MAPS Method." *Personnel,* 1974b, *51* (3), 35-47.

Kilmann, R. H. "Participative Management in the College

Classroom." *Journal of Applied Psychology,* 1974c, *59* (3), 337–338.

Kilmann, R. H. "Designing and Developing a 'Real' Organization in the Classroom." *Academy of Management Journal,* 1975a, *18* (1), 143–148.

Kilmann, R. H. "A Scaled-Projective Measure of Interpersonal Values." *Journal of Personality Assessment,* 1975b, *39* (1), 34–40.

Kilmann, R. H. *Social Systems Design: Normative Theory and the MAPS Design Technology.* New York: Elsevier North-Holland, 1977.

Kilmann, R. H. "On Integrating Knowledge Utilization with Knowledge Development: The Philosophy Behind the MAPS Design Technology." *Academy of Management Review,* 1979a, *4* (3), 417–426.

Kilmann, R. H. "Problem Management: A Behavioral Science Approach." In G. Zaltman (ed.), *Management Principles for Nonprofit Agencies and Organizations.* New York: American Management Association, 1979b.

Kilmann, R. H. "Organization Design for Knowledge Utilization." *Knowledge: Creation, Diffusion, Utilization,* 1981a, *3* (2), 211–231.

Kilmann, R. H. "Toward a Unique/Useful Concept of Values for Interpersonal Behavior: A Critical Review of the Literature on Value." *Psychological Reports,* 1981b, *48* (3), 939–959.

Kilmann, R. H. "Designing Collateral Organizations." *Human Systems Management,* 1982a, *3* (2), 66–76.

Kilmann, R. H. "Getting Control of the Corporate Culture." *Managing,* 1982b, *3*, 11–17.

Kilmann, R. H. "The Costs of Organization Structure: Dispelling the Myths of Independent Divisions and Organization-Wide Decision Making." *Accounting, Organizations, and Society,* 1983a, *8* (4), 341–357.

Kilmann, R. H. "A Dialectical Approach to Formulating and Testing Social Science Theories: Assumptional Analysis." *Human Relations,* 1983b, *36* (1), 1–22.

Kilmann, R. H. "A Typology of Organization Typologies: Toward Parsimony and Integration in the Organizational Sciences." *Human Relations,* 1983c, *36* (6), 523–548.

Kilmann, R. H. *Beyond the Quick Fix: Managing Five Tracks to Organizational Success.* San Francisco: Jossey-Bass, 1984a.

Kilmann, R. H. "Beyond the Quick Fix: Why Managers Must Disregard the Myth of Simplicity as a Direct Route to Organizational Success." *Management Review,* Nov. 1984b, pp. 24-28.

Kilmann, R. H. "Understanding Matrix Organization: Keeping the Dialectic Alive and Well." In D. D. Warrick (ed.), *Current Developments in Organization Development.* Glenview, Ill.: Scott, Foresman, 1984c.

Kilmann, R. H. "A Complete Program for Organizational Success." *Consultation,* 1985a, *4* (4), 316-330.

Kilmann, R. H. "Corporate Culture: Managing the Intangible Style of Corporate Life May Be the Key to Avoiding Stagnation." *Psychology Today,* Apr. 1985b, pp. 62-68.

Kilmann, R. H. "Managing All Barriers to Organizational Success." *Training and Development Journal,* 1985c, *39* (9), 64-72.

Kilmann, R. H. "Managing Troublemakers." *Training and Development Journal,* 1985d, *39* (5), 102-107.

Kilmann, R. H. "Organizational Success: Beyond the Quick Fix." *Administrative Radiology,* 1985e, *4* (6), 26-32.

Kilmann, R. H. "The Underground World of Corporate Culture." *The International Management Development Review,* 1987, *3,* 96-100.

Kilmann, R. H. "Change at the Top." *Strategic Direction,* Apr. 1988a, pp. 23-24.

Kilmann, R. H. "Management of Corporate Culture." In M. D. Fottler, S. R. Hernandez, and C. L. Joiner (eds.), *Strategic Management of Human Resources in Health Service Organizations.* New York: Wiley, 1988b.

Kilmann, R. H. "Paradoxical Interventions for Top Managers and Troublemakers." In R. E. Quinn and K. S. Cameron (eds.), *Paradox and Transformation: Towards a Theory of Change in Organization and Management.* Boston: Pitman, 1988c.

Kilmann, R. H., Benecki, T. J., and Shkop, Y. M. "Integrating the Benefits of Different Efforts at Management Consulting: The Case of Human Resources, Organization Development, and Organization Design." In G. J. Gore and R. G. Wright (eds.),

*The Academic/Consultant Connection.* Dubuque, Iowa: Kendall/Hunt, 1979.

Kilmann, R. H., Covin, T. J., and Associates. *Corporate Transformation: Revitalizing Organizations for a Competitive World.* San Francisco: Jossey-Bass, 1987.

Kilmann, R. H., and Ghymn, K. "The MAPS Design Technology: Designing Strategic Intelligence Systems for Multinational Corporations." *Columbia Journal of World Business,* 1976, *11* (2), 35-47.

Kilmann, R. H., and Herden, R. P. "Towards a Systemic Methodology for Evaluating the Impact of Interventions on Organizational Effectiveness." *Academy of Management Review,* 1976, *1* (3), 87-98.

Kilmann, R. H., and McKelvey, B. "The MAPS Route to Better Organization Design." *California Management Review,* 1975, *17* (3), 23-31.

Kilmann, R. H., and the MAPS Group. "MAPS as a Design Technology to Effectively Mobilize Resources for Social and Organization Problem Solving." In R. H. Kilmann, L. R. Pondy, and D. P. Slevin (eds.), *The Management of Organization Design.* Vol. 1: *Strategies and Implementation.* New York: Elsevier North-Holland, 1976.

Kilmann, R. H., and Mitroff, I. I. "Qualitative Versus Quantitative Analysis for Management Science: Different Forms for Different Psychological Types." *Interfaces,* 1976, *6* (2), 17-28.

Kilmann, R. H., and Mitroff, I. I. "Problem Defining and the Consulting/Intervention Process." *California Management Review,* 1979, *21* (3), 26-33.

Kilmann, R. H., Mitroff, I. I., and Lyles, M. A. "Designing an Effective Problem Solving Organization with the MAPS Design Technology." *Journal of Management,* 1976, *2* (2), 1-10.

Kilmann, R. H., Pondy, L. R., and Slevin, D. P. (eds.). *The Management of Organization Design.* Vol. 1: *Strategies and Implementation.* New York: Elsevier North-Holland, 1976a.

Kilmann, R. H., Pondy, L. R., and Slevin, D. P. (eds.). *The Management of Organization Design.* Vol. 2: *Research and Methodology.* New York: Elsevier North-Holland, 1976b.

Kilmann, R. H., and Saxton, M. J. *The Kilmann-Saxton Culture-*

*Gap Survey.* Pittsburgh, Pa.: Organizational Design Consultants, 1983.

Kilmann, R. H., Saxton, M. J., and Serpa, R. "Issues in Understanding and Changing Culture." *California Management Review,* 1986, *28* (2), 87-94.

Kilmann, R. H., Saxton, M. J., Serpa, R., and Associates. *Gaining Control of the Corporate Culture.* San Francisco: Jossey-Bass, 1985.

Kilmann, R. H., and Seltzer, J. "An Experimental Test of Organization Design Theory and the MAPS Design Technology: Homogeneous Versus Heterogeneous Composition of Organizational Subsystems." *Proceedings of the Eastern Academy of Management,* May 1976, pp. 93-97.

Kilmann, R. H., and Seltzer, J. "Laboratory Simulations with the MAPS Design Technology: The Effect of Subsystem Composition on Organizational Effectiveness." *Proceedings of the Southern Management Association,* Nov. 1978, pp. 139-141.

Kilmann, R. H., Slevin, D. P., and Thomas, K. W. "The Problem of Producing Useful Knowledge." In R. H. Kilmann and others (eds.), *Producing Useful Knowledge for Organizations.* New York: Praeger, 1983.

Kilmann, R. H., and Taylor, V. "A Contingency Approach to Laboratory Learning: Psychological Types Versus Experiential Norms." *Human Relations,* 1974, *27* (9), 891-909.

Kilmann, R. H., and Thomas, K. W. "Interpersonal Conflict-Handling Behavior as Reflections of Jungian Personality Dimensions." *Psychological Reports,* 1975, *37* (3), 971-980.

Kilmann, R. H., and Thomas, K. W. "Developing a Forced-Choice Measure of Conflict-Handling Behavior: The MODE Instrument." *Educational and Psychological Measurement,* 1977, *37* (2), 309-325.

Kilmann, R. H., and Thomas, K. W. "Four Perspectives on Conflict Management: An Attributional Framework for Organizing Descriptive and Normative Theory." *Academy of Management Review,* 1978, *3* (1), 59-68.

Kilmann, R. H., and others (eds.). *Producing Useful Knowledge for Organizations.* New York: Praeger, 1983.

King, W. R., Kilmann, R. H., and Sochats, K. "Designing Scientific

Journals: Issues and Survey Results." *Management Science,* 1978, *24* (1), 774–784.

"Kodak Reorganizes Photographic Division Along Business Lines." *Wall Street Journal,* Nov. 19, 1984, p. 22.

Lave, C. A., and March, J. G. *An Introduction to Models in the Social Sciences.* New York: Harper & Row, 1975.

Lawler, E. E., III. *Pay and Organizational Effectiveness: A Psychological View.* New York: McGraw-Hill, 1971.

Lawler, E. E., III. *Pay and Organization Development.* Reading, Mass.: Addison-Wesley, 1981.

Lawler, E. E., III. *High-Involvement Management: Participative Strategies for Improving Organizational Performance.* San Francisco: Jossey-Bass, 1986.

Lawrence, P. R., and Lorsch, J. W. *Organization and Environment.* Boston: Division of Research, Graduate School of Business Administration, Harvard University, 1967.

Leavitt, H. J. "Applied Organizational Change in Industry: Structural, Technological and Humanistic Approaches." In J. G. March (ed.), *Handbook of Organizations.* Chicago: Rand McNally, 1965.

Levinson, H. *Organizational Diagnosis.* Cambridge, Mass.: Harvard University Press, 1972.

Lewicki, R. "Organizational Seduction: Building Commitment to Organizations." *Organizational Dynamics,* Autumn 1981, pp. 5–21.

Lewin, K. *Field Theory in Social Science.* New York: Harper & Row, 1951.

Littlejohn, R. F. "Team Management: A How-to Approach to Improved Productivity, Higher Morale, and Longer-Lasting Job Satisfaction." *Management Review,* Jan. 1982, pp. 23–28.

Lombardo, M. M., and McCall, M. M., Jr. "The Intolerable Boss." *Psychology Today,* Jan. 1984, pp. 44–48.

McKelvey, B., and Kilmann, R. H. "Organization Design: A Participative Multivariate Approach." *Administrative Science Quarterly,* 1975, *20* (1), 24–36.

Mackenzie, K. D. *Organizational Structures.* Arlington Heights, Ill.: AHM Publishing, 1978.

Mackenzie, K. D. *Organizational Design: The Organizational Audit and Analysis Technology.* Norwood, N.J.: Ablex, 1986.

Main, J. "Trying to Bend Managers' Minds." *Fortune,* Nov. 23, 1987, pp. 95-107.

Marchione, A. R., and English, J. "Managing the Unpredictable— A Rational Plan for Coping with Change." *Management Review,* Feb. 1982, pp. 52-57.

Mason, R. O., and Mitroff, I. I. *Challenging Strategic Planning Assumptions: Theory, Cases, and Techniques.* New York: Wiley, 1981.

Mathis, R. L., and Jackson, J. H. *Personnel: Contemporary Perspectives and Applications.* (2nd ed.) St. Paul, Minn.: West, 1979.

Mayer, R. J. "Don't Be Hoodwinked by the Panacean Conspiracy." *Management Review,* June 1983, pp. 23-25.

Mendel, W. M. "Responsibility in Health, Illness, and Treatment." *Archives of General Psychiatry,* 1968, *10* (18), 697-705.

Meyer, H. H., Kay, E., and French, J.R.P., Jr. "Split Roles in Performance Appraisal." *Harvard Business Review,* Jan.-Feb. 1965, pp. 123-129.

Mitroff, I. I. *Stakeholders of the Organizational Mind: Toward a New View of Organizational Policy Making.* San Francisco: Jossey-Bass, 1983.

Mitroff, I. I., Barabba, V. P., and Kilmann, R. H. "The Application of Behavioral and Philosophical Technologies to Strategic Planning: A Case Study with a Large Federal Agency." *Management Science,* 1977, *24* (1), 44-58.

Mitroff, I. I., Emshoff, J. R., and Kilmann, R. H. "Assumptional Analysis: A Methodology for Strategic Problem Solving." *Management Science,* 1979, *25* (6), 583-593.

Mitroff, I. I., and Kilmann, R. H. "On Evaluating Scientific Research: The Contributions of the Psychology of Science." *Technological Forecasting and Social Change,* 1975a, *8* (4), 163-174.

Mitroff, I. I., and Kilmann, R. H. "Stories Managers Tell: A New Tool for Organizational Problem Solving." *Management Review,* 1975b, *64* (7), 18-28.

Mitroff, I. I., and Kilmann, R. H. "Systemic Knowledge: An

Integrated Program of Research on Science." *Theory and Society*, 1977a, *4* (1), 103–129.

Mitroff, I. I., and Kilmann, R. H. "Teaching Managers to Do Policy Analysis: The Case of Corporate Bribery." *California Management Review*, 1977b, *20* (1), 47–54.

Mitroff, I. I., and Kilmann, R. H. "On Integrating Behavioral and Philosophical Systems: Toward a Unified Theory of Problem Solving." In R. A. Jones (ed.), *Research in Sociology of Knowledge, Sciences, and Art*. Vol. 1. Greenwich, Conn.: JAI Press, 1978a.

Mitroff, I. I., and Kilmann, R. H. *Methodological Approaches to Social Science: Integrating Divergent Concepts and Theories*. San Francisco: Jossey-Bass, 1978b.

Mitroff, I. I., and Kilmann, R. H. "The Four-Fold Way of Knowing: The Varieties of Social Science Experience." *Theory and Society*, 1981, *10* (2), 227–248.

Mitroff, I. I., and Kilmann, R. H. "Intellectual Resistance to Useful Knowledge: An Archetypal Social Analysis." In R. H. Kilmann and others (eds.), *Producing Useful Knowledge for Organizations*. New York: Praeger, 1983.

Mitroff, I. I., and Kilmann, R. H. *Corporate Tragedies: Product Tampering, Sabotage, and Other Catastrophes*. New York: Praeger, 1984a.

Mitroff, I. I., and Kilmann, R. H. "Corporate Tragedies: Teaching Companies to Cope with Evil." *New Management*, 1984b, *1* (4), 48–53.

Mitroff, I. I., and Kilmann, R. H. "Companies Must Design Mechanisms to Cope with Unforeseen Disaster." *Los Angeles Times*, Apr. 28, 1985a, p. 3.

Mitroff, I. I., and Kilmann, R. H. "Why Corporate Disasters Are on the Increase, and How Companies Can Cope with Them." *Public Affairs Review*, 1985b, *6*, 5–21.

Mitroff, I. I., and Kilmann, R. H. "Will Bhopal Happen Again?" *Management Review*, Sept. 1985c, pp. 61–62.

Mitroff, I. I., Kilmann, R. H., and Barabba, V. P. "Avoiding the Design of Management Misinformation Systems: A Strategic Approach." In G. Zaltman (ed.), *Management Principles for*

*Nonprofit Agencies and Organizations.* New York: American Management Association, 1979.

Moch, M., and Seashore, S. E. "How Norms Affect Behaviors in and of Corporations." In P. C. Nystrom and W. H. Starbuck (eds.), *Handbook of Organizational Design.* London: Oxford University Press, 1981.

Myers, I. B. *Myers-Briggs Type Indicator.* Princeton, N.J.: Educational Testing Service, 1962.

Myers, I. B. *Myers-Briggs Type Indicator.* Palo Alto, Calif.: Consulting Psychologists Press, 1978.

Naisbitt, J. *Megatrends: Ten New Directions Transforming Our Lives.* New York: Warner Books, 1984.

Nystrom, P. C., and Starbuck, W. H. "To Avoid Organizational Crises, Unlearn." *Organizational Dynamics,* Spring 1984, pp. 53–65.

O'Toole, J. *Making America Work: Productivity and Responsibility.* New York: Continuum, 1981.

O'Toole, J. "Declining Innovation: The Failure of Success, a Summary Report of the Seventh Twenty-Year Forecast Project." Los Angeles: Center for Futures Research, Graduate School of Business, University of Southern California, Los Angeles, 1983.

Ouchi, W. *Theory Z: How American Business Can Meet the Japanese Challenge.* Reading, Mass.: Addison-Wesley, 1981.

Pascale, R., and Athos, A. *The Art of Japanese Management.* New York: Simon & Schuster, 1981.

Paulson, R. D. "The Chief Executive as Change Agent." *Management Review,* Feb. 1982, pp. 25–28, 41–42.

Peter, L. J., and Hull, R. *The Peter Principle.* New York: Morrow, 1969.

Peters, T. J., and Waterman, R. H., Jr. *In Search of Excellence: Lessons from America's Best-Run Companies.* New York: Harper & Row, 1982.

"Photo Division Reorganized on Line-of-Business Basis." *Kodakery,* Nov. 16, 1984, pp. 1–8.

Popper, K. R. *The Logic of Scientific Discovery.* London: Hutchinson, 1959.

Porter, L. W., and Lawler, E. E., III. *Managerial Attitudes and Performance.* Homewood, Ill.: Irwin-Dorsey, 1968.

Porter, L. W., Lawler, E. E., III, and Hackman, J. R. *Behavior in Organizations*. New York: McGraw-Hill, 1975.

Porter, M. E. *Competitive Advantage: Creating and Sustaining Superior Performance*. New York: Free Press, 1985.

Rose, F. "The Mass Production of Engineers." *Esquire*, May 1983, pp. 76–84.

Rosen, E., Fox, R. E., and Gregory, I. *Abnormal Psychology*. (2nd ed.) Philadelphia: Saunders, 1972.

Rotter, J. B. "External Control and Internal Control." *Psychology Today*, June 1971, pp. 37–42, 58–59.

Salmans, S. "New Vogue: Company Culture." *New York Times*, Jan. 7, 1983, pp. D1, D27.

Sashkin, M. "Participative Management Is an Ethical Imperative." *Organizational Dynamics*, Spring 1984, pp. 5–22.

Schein, E. H. *Process Consultation: Its Role in Organization Development*. Reading, Mass.: Addison-Wesley, 1969.

Schein, E. H. *Organizational Culture and Leadership: A Dynamic View*. San Francisco: Jossey-Bass, 1985.

Schwartz, H., and Davis, S. M. "Matching Corporate Culture and Business Strategy." *Organizational Dynamics*, Summer 1981, pp. 30–48.

Seashore, S. E. *Group Cohesiveness in the Industrial Work Group*. Ann Arbor, Mich.: Institute for Social Research, 1954.

Seltzer, J., and Kilmann, R. H. "Effect of Group Composition on Group Process: Homogeneity Versus Heterogeneity on Task and People Dimensions." *Psychological Reports*, 1977, *41* (3), 1195–1200.

Serpa, R. "Why Many Organizations—Despite Good Intentions— Often Fail to Give Employees Fair and Useful Performance Reviews." *Management Review*, 1984, *73* (7), 41–45.

Slater, P. *Earthwalk*. New York: Anchor/Doubleday, 1974.

Thomas, K. W., and Kilmann, R. H. *Thomas-Kilmann Conflict MODE Instrument*. New York: XICOM, 1974.

Thomas, K. W., and Kilmann, R. H. "The Social Desirability Variable in Organizational Research: An Alternative Explanation for Reported Findings." *Academy of Management Journal*, 1975, *18* (4), 471–482.

Thomas, K. W., and Kilmann, R. H. "Comparison of Four

Instruments Measuring Conflict Behavior." *Psychological Reports,* 1978, *42* (3), 1139–1145.

Thompson, J. D. *Organizations in Action.* New York: McGraw-Hill, 1967.

Tichy, N. M. *Managing Strategic Change: Technical, Political, and Cultural Dynamics.* New York: Wiley, 1983.

Toffler, A. *Future Shock.* New York: Bantam Books, 1970.

Toffler, A. *The Third Wave.* New York: Morrow, 1980.

Tomasko, R. M. "Managing Compensation Strategically: Focusing Company Reward Systems to Help Achieve Business Objectives." *Management Review,* Oct. 1982, pp. 8–12.

Wallach, E. J. "Individuals and Organizations: The Cultural Match." *Training and Development Journal,* Feb. 1983, pp. 29–36.

Walton, R. E. *Interpersonal Peacemaking: Confrontations and Third Party Consultation.* Reading, Mass.: Addison-Wesley, 1969.

Weinshall, T. D. "Help for Chief Executives: The Outside Consultant." *California Management Review,* 1982, *24* (4), 47–58.

Yankelovich, D. *New Rules: Search for Self-Fulfillment in a World Turned Upside Down.* New York: Random House, 1981.

Zand, D. E. *Information, Organization, and Power.* New York: McGraw-Hill, 1981.

# Index